Macbeth

and Related Readings

McDougal Littell
A HOUGHTON MIFFLIN COMPANY

Evanston, Illinois   *Boston*   *Dallas*

Acknowledgments

New Directions Publishing Corp.: "Insomniac," from *Collected Poems 1957–1987* by Octavio Paz. Copyright © 1986 by Octavio Paz and Eliot Weinberger. Reprinted by permission of New Directions Publishing Corp.

Random House, Inc.: "Better Than Counting Sheep," from *Being Here: Poetry 1977–1980* by Robert Penn Warren. Copyright © 1978, 1979, 1980 by Robert Penn Warren. Reprinted by permission of Random House, Inc.

Penguin Books USA Inc.: "Macbeth," from *The Friendly Shakespeare* by Norrie Epstein; Copyright © 1993 by Norrie Epstein, Jon Winokur, and Reid Boates. Reprinted by permission of Viking Penguin, a division of Penguin Books USA Inc.

Leila Vennewitz and Verlag Kiepenheuer & Witsch: "Like a Bad Dream," from *Heinrich Böll: 18 Stories* by Heinrich Böll, translated by Leila Vennewitz; Copyright © 1966 by Heinrich Böll. Reprinted by permission of Leila Vennewitz and Verlag Kiepenheuer & Witsch, c/o Joan Daves Agency as agent for the proprietor.

Samuel French, Inc.: *How Many Children Had Lady Macbeth* by Don Nigro; Copyright © 1989 by Don Nigro. Reprinted by permission of Samuel French, Inc.

The New Statesman: "Into concrete mixer throw" by Barbara Roe. Reprinted by permission of The New Statesman.

Georges Borchardt, Inc.: "Yscolan" by Myrrdyn, from *Selected Translations 1948–1968*, edited and translated by W. S. Merwin; Copyright © 1962 by W. S. Merwin. Reprinted by permission of Georges Borchardt, Inc.

Cover illustration by Alexander Barsky.
Cover background credit: Top: Copyright © Diane Meredith.
Author photo: North Wind Picture Archives.

ISBN 0-395-77553-1

7—DCI—02 01 00

Contents

Continued

Macbeth

William Shakespeare

Characters

Duncan, King of Scotland

HIS SONS

Malcolm

Donalbain

GENERALS OF THE SCOTTISH ARMY

Macbeth

Banquo

NOBLEMEN OF SCOTLAND

Macduff

Lennox

Ross

Menteith (men tēth')

Angus

Caithness (kāth' nis)

Fleance (flā' äns), son of Banquo

Siward (sē' wurd), Earl of Northumberland, General of the English forces

Young Siward, his son

Seyton (sā' tən), an Officer attending on Macbeth

Boy, son of Macduff

A Captain

An English Doctor

A Scottish Doctor

A Porter

An Old Man

Lady Macbeth

Lady Macduff

A Gentlewoman attending on Lady Macbeth

Hecate (hek′ ət), goddess of witchcraft

Three Witches

The Ghost of Banquo

Apparitions

Lords, Gentlemen, Officers, Soldiers, Murderers, Messengers, Attendants

The Time: The eleventh century

The Place: Scotland and England

3 *hurlyburly:* turmoil; uproar.

9-10 *Graymalkin . . . Paddock:* two demon helpers in the form of a cat and a toad.

11 *Anon:* immediately.

12 *Fair . . . fair:* The witches delight in the confusion of good and bad, beauty and ugliness.

Exeunt (*Latin*): Everyone leaves the stage.

ONE

Scene 1 *An open place in Scotland.*

The play opens in a wild and lonely place in medieval Scotland. Three witches enter and speak of what they know will happen this day: The civil war will end, and they will meet Macbeth, one of the generals. Their meeting ends when their demon companions, in the form of a toad and a cat, call them away.

[Thunder and lightning. Enter three Witches.*]*

First Witch. When shall we three meet again
  In thunder, lightning, or in rain?

Second Witch. When the hurlyburly's done,
  When the battle's lost and won.

5 **Third Witch.** That will be ere the set of sun.

First Witch. Where the place?

Second Witch.   Upon the heath.

Third Witch. There to meet with Macbeth.

First Witch. I come, Graymalkin!

10 **Second Witch.** Paddock calls.

Third Witch.   Anon!

All. Fair is foul, and foul is fair.
  Hover through the fog and filthy air.

[Exeunt.]

Alarum within: the sound of a trumpet offstage, a signal that soldiers should arm themselves.

1-3 Because of the confusion of battle, Duncan does not know who is winning. To find out, he calls on a bloody soldier, whose condition (**plight**) shows recent fighting.

6 **'Gainst my captivity:** to save me from capture.

7 **broil:** battle.

9-11 **Doubtful . . . art:** The two armies are compared to two exhausted swimmers who cling to each other and thus cannot swim.

11-17 The officer hates Macdonwald, a rebel whose evils (**multiplying villainies**) swarm like insects around him. His army consists of soldiers (**kerns and gallowglasses**) from the Hebrides, islands off the west coast of Scotland. Fortune, traditionally depicted as a fickle woman, has smiled upon him, giving him temporary success.

21 **valor's minion:** the favorite of valor, meaning the bravest of all.

Scene 2 *King Duncan's camp near the battlefield.*

Duncan, the king of Scotland, waits in his camp for news of the battle. He learns that one of his generals, Macbeth, has been victorious in several battles. Not only has Macbeth defeated the rebellious Macdonwald, but he has also conquered the armies of the king of Norway and the Scottish traitor, the thane of Cawdor. Duncan orders the thane of Cawdor's execution and announces that Macbeth will receive the traitor's title.

[Alarum within. Enter Duncan, Malcolm, Donalbain, Lennox, with Attendants, meeting a bleeding Captain.]

Duncan. What bloody man is that? He can report,
As seemeth by his plight, of the revolt
The newest state.

Malcolm.   This is the sergeant
5   Who like a good and hardy soldier fought
'Gainst my captivity. Hail, brave friend!
Say to the King the knowledge of the broil
As thou didst leave it.

Captain.   Doubtful it stood,
10   As two spent swimmers that do cling together
And choke their art. The merciless Macdonwald
(Worthy to be a rebel, for to that
The multiplying villainies of nature
Do swarm upon him) from the Western Isles
15   Of kerns and gallowglasses is supplied;
And Fortune, on his damned quarrel smiling,
Showed like a rebel's whore. But all's too weak;
For brave Macbeth (well he deserves that name),
Disdaining Fortune, with his brandished steel,
20   Which smoked with bloody execution
(Like valor's minion), carved out his passage
Till he faced the slave;
Which ne'er shook hands nor bade farewell to him

24 *unseamed him . . . chops:* split him open from the navel to the jaw. *What does this act suggest about Macbeth?*

26 *cousin:* Duncan and Macbeth are first cousins.

27-30 *As whence . . . discomfort swells:* As the rising sun is sometimes followed by storms, a new assault on Macbeth began.

32 *to trust their heels:* to retreat quickly.

33-35 *the Norweyan . . . assault:* The King of Norway took an opportunity to attack.

40 *sooth:* the truth.

41 *double cracks:* a double load of ammunition.

43-44 *Except . . . memorize another Golgotha:* The officer's admiration leads to exaggeration. He claims he cannot decide whether (*except*) Macbeth and Banquo wanted to bathe in blood or make the battlefield as famous as Golgotha, the site of Christ's crucifixion.

50 *Thane:* a Scottish noble, similar in rank to an English earl.

Till he unseamed him from the nave to the chops
25   And fixed his head upon our battlements.

Duncan. O valiant cousin! worthy gentleman!

Captain. As whence the sun 'gins his reflection
Shipwracking storms and direful thunders break,
So from that spring whence comfort seemed to come
30   Discomfort swells. Mark, King of Scotland, mark.
No sooner justice had, with valor armed,
Compelled these skipping kerns to trust their heels
But the Norweyan lord, surveying vantage,
With furbished arms and new supplies of men,
35   Began a fresh assault.

Duncan.   Dismayed not this
Our captains, Macbeth and Banquo?

Captain.   Yes,
As sparrows eagles, or the hare the lion.
40   If I say sooth, I must report they were
As cannons overcharged with double cracks, so they
Doubly redoubled strokes upon the foe.
Except they meant to bathe in reeking wounds,
Or memorize another Golgotha,
45   I cannot tell—
But I am faint; my gashes cry for help.

Duncan. So well thy words become thee as thy wounds
They smack of honor both. Go get him surgeons.

[Exit Captain, attended.]

[Enter Ross and Angus.]

Who comes here?

50   **Malcolm.**   The worthy Thane of Ross.

Lennox. What a haste looks through his eyes! So
          should he look
That seems to speak things strange.

Ross.   God save the King!

56-66 Ross has arrived from Fife, where Norway's troops had invaded and frightened the people. There the King of Norway, along with the Scottish traitor the Thane of Cawdor, met Macbeth (described as the husband of **Bellona**, the goddess of war). Macbeth, in heavy armor (**proof**), challenged the enemy, matched his strength, and achieved victory.

69 *craves composition:* wants a treaty.

70 *deign:* allow.

71 *disbursed, at Saint Colme's Inch:* paid at Saint Colme's Inch, an island in the North Sea between Norway and Scotland.

73-74 *deceive / our bosom interest:* betray our affections or friendship; *present death:* immediate execution.

75 *What reward has the king decided to give to Macbeth?*

55 **Duncan.** Whence cam'st thou, worthy thane?

Ross.   From Fife, great King,
   Where the Norweyan banners flout the sky
   And fan our people cold. Norway himself,
   With terrible numbers,
60 Assisted by that most disloyal traitor
   The Thane of Cawdor, began a dismal conflict,
   Till that Bellona's bridegroom, lapped in proof,
   Confronted him with self-comparisons,
   Point against point, rebellious arm 'gainst arm,
65 Curbing his lavish spirit; and to conclude,
   The victory fell on us.

Duncan.   Great happiness!

Ross.   That now
   Sweno, the Norways' king, craves composition;
70 Nor would we deign him burial of his men
   Till he disbursed, at Saint Colme's Inch,
   Ten thousand dollars to our general use.

Duncan. No more that Thane of Cawdor shall deceive
   Our bosom interest. Go pronounce his present death
75 And with his former title greet Macbeth.

Ross. I'll see it done.

Duncan. What he hath lost noble Macbeth hath won.

[Exeunt.]

Scene 3 *A bleak place near the battlefield.*

   *While leaving the battlefield, Macbeth and
   Banquo meet the witches, who are gleefully
   discussing the trouble they have caused. The
   witches hail Macbeth by a title he already
   holds, thane of Glamis. Then they prophesy
   that he will become both thane of Cawdor and
   king. When Banquo asks about his future, they
   speak in riddles, saying that he will be the
   father of kings but not a king himself.*

2 *Killing swine:* Witches were often accused of killing people's pigs.

5 *mounched:* munched.

7 *"Aroint thee, witch!" . . . ronyon cries:* "Go away, witch!" the fat-bottomed (*rump-fed*), ugly creature (*ronyon*) cries.

8-10 The woman's husband, the master of a merchant ship (*the "Tiger"*), has sailed to Aleppo, a famous trading center in the Middle East. The witch will pursue him. Witches, who could change shape at will, were thought to sail on strainers (*sieve*).

16-25 The witch is going to torture the woman's husband. She has control of the winds and all the places where they blow, covering all points of a compass (*shipman's card*). She will make him sleepless, keeping his eyelids (penthouse lid) from closing. Thus, he will lead an accursed (*forbid*) life for weeks (*sev'nights*) and weeks, wasting away with fatigue.

*After the witches vanish, Ross and Angus
arrive to announce that Macbeth has been
named thane of Cawdor. The first part of the
witches' prophecy has come true, and
Macbeth is stunned. He immediately begins to
consider the possibility of murdering King
Duncan to fulfill the rest of the witches'
prophecy to him. Shaken, he turns his
thoughts away from this "horrid image."*

[*Thunder. Enter the three* Witches.]

First Witch. Where hast thou been, sister?

Second Witch. Killing swine.

Third Witch. Sister, where thou?

First Witch. A sailor's wife had chestnuts in her lap
5   And mounched and mounched and mounched.
      "Give me," quoth I.
    "Aroint thee, witch!" the rump-fed ronyon cries.
    Her husband's to Aleppo gone, master o' the
      "Tiger";
10   But in a sieve I'll thither sail
    And, like a rat without a tail,
    I'll do, I'll do, and I'll do.

Second Witch. I'll give thee a wind.

First Witch. Th' art kind.

15 **Third Witch.** And I another.

First Witch. I myself have all the other,
    And the very ports they blow,
    All the quarters that they know
    I' the shipman's card.
20   I'll drain him dry as hay.
    Sleep shall neither night nor day
    Hang upon his penthouse lid.
    He shall live a man forbid.
    Weary sev'nights, nine times nine,

26-31 Though she lacks the power to sink his ship (***bark***), she'll toss it in the wind. Finally, she brags about having a bone (***pilot's thumb***) to aid her magic.

35 ***posters:*** quick riders.

38 Nine was considered a magical number by superstitious people.

44-50 ***aught:*** anything; ***choppy:*** chapped; ***your beards:*** Beards on women identified them as witches. Banquo vividly describes the witches. *What does he notice about them?*

52-57 *What is surprising about the three titles the witches use to greet Macbeth?*

25 Shall he dwindle, peak, and pine.
Though his bark cannot be lost,
Yet it shall be tempest-tost.
Look what I have.

Second Witch. Show me! Show me!

30 **First Witch.** Here I have a pilot's thumb,
Wracked as homeward he did come.

[Drum within.]

Third Witch. A drum, a drum!
Macbeth doth come.

All. The Weird Sisters, hand in hand,
35 Posters of the sea and land,
Thus do go about, about,
Thrice to thine, and thrice to mine,
And thrice again, to make up nine.
Peace! The charm's wound up.

[Enter Macbeth and Banquo.]

40 **Macbeth.** So foul and fair a day I have not seen.
Banquo. How far is't called to Forres? What are these,
So withered, and so wild in their attire,
That look not like the inhabitants o' the earth,
And yet are on't? Live you? or are you aught
45 That man may question? You seem to understand
me,
By each at once her choppy finger laying
Upon her skinny lips. You should be women,
And yet your beards forbid me to interpret
50 That you are so.

Macbeth.   Speak, if you can. What are you?

First Witch. All hail, Macbeth! Hail to thee, Thane of
Glamis!

Second Witch. All hail, Macbeth! Hail to thee, Thane
55   of Cawdor!

60 ***Are ye fantastical:*** Are you (the witches) imaginary?

61-64 ***My noble partner . . . rapt withal:*** The witches' prophecies of noble possessions (***having***)—the lands and wealth of Cawdor—and kingship (***royal hopes***) have left Macbeth dazed (***rapt withal***). Look for evidence that shows what Macbeth thinks of the prophecies.

\

72-75 The witches speak in riddles. Though Banquo will be less fortunate (***happy***) than Macbeth, he will be father to (***get***) future kings. *What do the witches predict for Banquo? What do you think their predictions mean?*

78-82 Macbeth knows he is Thane of Glamis, since the title passed to him when his father, ***Sinel,*** died. Thus, the witches' first "prediction" is true. He questions the other two titles, however, since he does not know that he has been named Thane of Cawdor by the King and, as he says, the idea of being king himself is beyond belief.

83-84 ***whence:*** where. Macbeth wants to know where the witches received their knowledge (***strange intelligence***).

Third Witch. All hail, Macbeth, that shalt be King
    hereafter!

Banquo. Good sir, why do you start and seem to fear
    Things that do sound so fair? I' the name of truth,
60   Are ye fantastical, or that indeed
    Which outwardly ye show? My noble partner
    You greet with present grace and great prediction
    Of noble having and of royal hope,
    That he seems rapt withal. To me you speak not.
65   If you can look into the seeds of time
    And say which grain will grow and which will not,
    Speak then to me, who neither beg nor fear
    Your favors nor your hate.

First Witch. Hail!

70 **Second Witch.** Hail!

Third Witch. Hail!

First Witch. Lesser than Macbeth, and greater.

Second Witch. Not so happy, yet much happier.

Third Witch. Thou shalt get kings, though thou be
75   none.
    So all hail, Macbeth and Banquo!

First Witch. Banquo and Macbeth, all hail!

Macbeth. Stay, you imperfect speakers, tell me more!
    By Sinel's death I know I am Thane of Glamis,
80   But how of Cawdor? The Thane of Cawdor lives,
    A prosperous gentleman; and to be King
    Stands not within the prospect of belief,
    No more than to be Cawdor. Say from whence
    You owe this strange intelligence, or why
85   Upon this blasted heath you stop our way
    With such prophetic greeting. Speak, I charge you.

[Witches *vanish.*]

88 *whither:* where.

89 *corporal:* physical, real.

94 *insane root:* A number of plants were believed to cause insanity when eaten.

103-104 *His wonders . . . Silenced with that:* King Duncan hesitates between awe (*wonders*) and gratitude (*praise*), and is, as a result, speechless.

107-108 *Nothing afeard . . . didst make:* Although Macbeth left many dead (*Strange images of death*), he obviously did not fear death himself.

109 *post with post:* messenger after messenger.

114 *herald thee:* They will act as heralds, ushering him in to Duncan.

116 *earnest:* partial payment.

118 *addition:* title.

Banquo. The earth hath bubbles, as the water has,
    And these are of them. Whither are they vanished?

Macbeth. Into the air, and what seemed corporal melted
90   As breath into the wind. Would they had stayed!

Banquo. Were such things here as we do speak about?
    Or have we eaten on the insane root
95   That takes the reason prisoner?

Macbeth. Your children shall be kings.

Banquo.   You shall be King.

Macbeth. And Thane of Cawdor too. Went it not so?

Banquo. To the selfsame tune and words. Who's here?

[Enter Ross and Angus.]

100 **Ross.** The King hath happily received, Macbeth,
    The news of thy success; and when he reads
    Thy personal venture in the rebels' fight,
    His wonders and his praises do contend
    Which should be thine or his. Silenced with that,
105   In viewing o'er the rest o' the selfsame day,
    He finds thee in the stout Norweyan ranks,
    Nothing afeard of what thyself didst make,
    Strange images of death. As thick as hail
    Came post with post, and every one did bear
110   Thy praises in his kingdom's great defense
    And poured them down before him.

Angus.   We are sent
    To give thee from our royal master thanks;
    Only to herald thee into his sight,
115   Not pay thee.

Ross. And for an earnest of a greater honor,
    He bade me, from him, call thee Thane of Cawdor;
    In which addition, hail, most worthy Thane!
    For it is thine.

120-123 Notice the contrast between the reactions of Macbeth and Banquo to the news of Macbeth's new title. Their differences will become more apparent later.

126-132 *Whether he was . . . overthrown him:* The former Thane of Cawdor may have been secretly allied (*combined*) with the King of Norway, or he may have supported the traitor Macdonwald (*did line the rebel*). But he is clearly guilty of treasons that deserve the death penalty (*capital treasons*), having aimed at the country's ruin (*wrack*).

133 *Aside:* a stage direction that means Macbeth is speaking to himself, beyond the hearing of others.

134 *behind:* to follow; next in line. *What is Macbeth referring to in this aside?*

140 *home:* fully; completely.

141 *enkindle you unto:* set on fire your hopes for; inflame your ambitions.

143-146 *to win us . . . consequence:* Banquo warns that evil powers often offer little truths to tempt people. The witches may be lying about what matters most (*in deepest consequence*).

148-150 *Two truths . . . imperial theme:* The first two "prophecies" only set the stage for the more important act of becoming king.

151-163 Macbeth separates himself from the others, his head spinning. Are the witches' predictions good or evil (*ill*)? If they are evil, why have two of them already proved true? If they are good, why is he suddenly filled with the terrible thought (*suggestion*) of killing King Duncan to make the third prediction come true? This idea (*horrible imaginings*) is more frightful than any fears justified by reality (*present fears*). Macbeth is so overwhelmed that his mind and body together (*single state of man*) are overcome by speculation (surmise) about the future. Nothing seems real but his imaginings (*what is not*).

Banquo. What, can the devil speak true?

Macbeth. The Thane of Cawdor lives. Why do you dress me
    In borrowed robes?

Angus. Who was the Thane lives yet,
But under heavy judgment bears that life
Which he deserves to lose. Whether he was combined
With those of Norway, or did line the rebel
With hidden help and vantage, or that with both
He labored in his country's wrack, I know not;
But treasons capital, confessed and proved,
Have overthrown him.

Macbeth. [Aside] Glamis, and Thane of Cawdor!
The greatest is behind.—[To Ross and Angus] Thanks
    for your pains.
[Aside to Banquo] Do you not hope your children
    shall be kings,
When those that gave the Thane of Cawdor to me
Promised no less to them?

Banquo. [Aside to Macbeth] That, trusted home,
Might yet enkindle you unto the crown,
Besides the Thane of Cawdor. But 'tis strange!
And oftentimes, to win us to our harm,
The instruments of darkness tell us truths,
Win us with honest trifles, to betray's
In deepest consequence.—
Cousins, a word, I pray you.

Macbeth. [Aside] Two truths are told,
As happy prologues to the swelling act
Of the imperial theme.—I thank you, gentlemen.—
[Aside] This supernatural soliciting
Cannot be ill; cannot be good. If ill,
Why hath it given me earnest of success,
Commencing in a truth? I am Thane of Cawdor.

120

125

130

135

140

145

150

167 *my stir:* my doing anything.

169-170 Banquo excuses Macbeth's odd behavior by comparing his new honors to new (*strange*) clothes that only become comfortable with wear.

171-172 *Come what . . . roughest day:* the future will arrive no matter what.

173 *stay:* wait.

176-178 *your pains . . . read them:* I will always remember your efforts. The metaphor refers to keeping a diary and reading it regularly.

180-182 *at more time . . . other:* Macbeth wants to discuss the prophecies later, after he and Banquo have had time to think about them.

155 If good, why do I yield to that suggestion
Whose horrid image doth unfix my hair
And make my seated heart knock at my ribs
Against the use of nature? Present fears
Are less than horrible imaginings.
160 My thought, whose murder yet is but fantastical,
Shakes so my single state of man that function
Is smothered in surmise and nothing is
But what is not.

Banquo.   Look how our partner's rapt.

165 **Macbeth.** *[Aside]* If chance will have me King, why,
     chance may crown me,
Without my stir.

Banquo.   New honors come upon him,
Like our strange garments, cleave not to their mold
170 But with the aid of use.

Macbeth.   *[Aside]* Come what come may,
Time and the hour runs through the roughest day.

Banquo. Worthy Macbeth, we stay upon your leisure.

Macbeth. Give me your favor. My dull brain was
175   wrought
With things forgotten. Kind gentlemen, your pains
Are registered where every day I turn
The leaf to read them. Let us toward the King.
[Aside to Banquo*]* Think upon what hath chanced, and,
180   at more time,
The interim having weighed it, let us speak
Our free hearts each to other.

Banquo. *[Aside to* Macbeth*]* Very gladly.

Macbeth. *[Aside to* Banquo*]* Till then, enough.—Come,
     friends.

[Exeunt.]

2 ***Those in commission:*** those who have the responsibility for Cawdor's execution.

7 ***set forth:*** showed.

9-12 ***He died as . . . trifle:*** He died as if he had rehearsed (***studied***) the moment. Though losing his life (***the dearest thing he owed***), he behaved with calm dignity.

17-24 ***O worthiest . . . pay:*** The King feels that he cannot repay (***recompense***) Macbeth enough. Macbeth's qualities and accomplishments are of greater value than any thanks or payment Duncan can give.

Scene 4 *A room in the king's palace at Forres.*

King Duncan receives news of the execution of the former thane of Cawdor. As the king is admitting his bad judgment concerning the traitor, Macbeth enters with Banquo, Ross, and Angus. Duncan expresses his gratitude to them and then, in a most unusual action, officially names his own son Malcolm as heir to the throne. To honor Macbeth, Duncan decides to visit Macbeth's castle at Inverness. Macbeth, his thoughts full of dark ambition, leaves to prepare for the king's visit.

[Flourish. Enter Duncan, Lennox, Malcolm, Donalbain, *and* Attendants.*]*

Duncan. Is execution done on Cawdor? Are not
    Those in commission yet returned?

Malcolm.   My liege,
    They are not yet come back. But I have spoke
5   With one that saw him die; who did report
    That very frankly he confessed his treasons,
    Implored your Highness' pardon, and set forth
    A deep repentance. Nothing in his life
    Became him like the leaving it. He died
10   As one that had been studied in his death
    To throw away the dearest thing he owed
    As 'twere a careless trifle.

Duncan.   There's no art
    To find the mind's construction in the face.
15   He was a gentleman on whom I built
    An absolute trust.

[Enter Macbeth, Banquo, Ross, *and* Angus.*]*

                  O worthiest cousin,
    The sin of my ingratitude even now
    Was heavy on me! Thou art so far before
20   That swiftest wing of recompense is slow
    To overtake thee. Would thou hadst less deserved,

25-30 *How does Macbeth respond to the King? Do you think his words match his thoughts? Why or why not?*

32-33 *I have . . . growing:* The King plans to give more honors to Macbeth. *What might Macbeth be thinking now?*

39-41 *My plenteous . . . sorrow:* The King is crying tears of joy.

45 *Prince of Cumberland:* the title given to the heir to the Scottish throne. Now that Malcolm is heir, Macbeth's chances of becoming king seem reduced. *How might Macbeth react to this unexpected twist?*

47 *signs of nobleness:* titles and honors.

48 *Inverness:* site of Macbeth's castle, where the King has just invited himself, giving another honor to Macbeth.

51 *harbinger:* a representative sent before a royal party to make proper arrangements for its arrival.

That the proportion both of thanks and payment
Might have been mine! Only I have left to say,
More is thy due than more than all can pay.

25 **Macbeth.** The service and the loyalty I owe,
In doing it pays itself. Your Highness' part
Is to receive our duties; and our duties
Are to your throne and state children and servants,
Which do but what they should by doing everything
30 Safe toward your love and honor.

Duncan.   Welcome hither.
I have begun to plant thee and will labor
To make thee full of growing. Noble Banquo,
That hast no less deserved, nor must be known
35 No less to have done so, let me infold thee
And hold thee to my heart.

Banquo.   There if I grow,
The harvest is your own.

Duncan.   My plenteous joys,
40 Wanton in fullness, seek to hide themselves
In drops of sorrow. Sons, kinsmen, thanes,
And you whose places are the nearest, know
We will establish our estate upon
Our eldest, Malcolm, whom we name hereafter
45 The Prince of Cumberland; which honor must
Not unaccompanied invest him only,
But signs of nobleness, like stars, shall shine
On all deservers. From hence to Inverness,
And bind us further to you.

50 **Macbeth.** The rest is labor, which is not used for you.
I'll be myself the harbinger, and make joyful
The hearing of my wife with your approach;
So, humbly take my leave.

Duncan.   My worthy Cawdor!

55 **Macbeth.** *[Aside]* The Prince of Cumberland! That is a
step

58-59 *Stars . . . desires:* Macbeth wants to hide his murderous thoughts.

60-61 *The eye . . . to see:* Macbeth hopes for the King's murder, although he does not want to see it.

62-66 Duncan continues an earlier conversation with Banquo about Macbeth's merits.

1-13 Lady Macbeth is reading a letter from her husband that recounts his meeting with the witches.

On which I must fall down, or else o'erleap,
For in my way it lies. Stars, hide your fires!
Let not light see my black and deep desires.
60 The eye wink at the hand; yet let that be,
Which the eye fears, when it is done, to see. *[Exit.]*

Duncan. True, worthy Banquo: he is full so valiant,
And in his commendations I am fed;
It is a banquet to me. Let's after him,
65 Whose care is gone before to bid us welcome.
It is a peerless kinsman.

[Flourish. Exeunt.]

Scene 5 *Macbeth's castle at Inverness.*

*Lady Macbeth reads a letter from her husband
that tells her of the witches' prophecies, one
of which has already come true. She is
determined that Macbeth will be king.
However, she fears that he lacks the courage
to kill Duncan. After a messenger tells her the
king is coming, she calls on the powers of evil
to help her do what must be done. When
Macbeth arrives, she tells him that the king
must die that night but reminds him that he
must appear to be a good and loyal host.*

[Enter Lady Macbeth *alone, with a letter.]*

Lady Macbeth. *[Reads]* "They met me in the day of
success; and I have learned by the perfect'st report they
have more in them than mortal knowledge. When I
burned in desire to question them further, they made
5 themselves air, into which they vanished. Whiles I stood
rapt in the wonder of it, came missives from the King,
who all-hailed me Thane of Cawdor, by which title,
before, these Weird Sisters saluted me, and referred me
to the coming on of time with 'Hail, King that shalt
10 be!' This have I thought good to deliver thee, my

16-31 *Yet do . . . withal:* Lady Macbeth fears her husband is too good (***too full o' the milk of human kindness***) to seize the throne by murder (***the nearest way***). Lacking the necessary wickedness (***illness***), he wants to gain power virtuously (***holily***). But she is convinced he would like to be king, even if becoming king requires murder (***that which rather thou dost fear to do***). She wishes him home (***Hie thee hither***) so that she can drive out (***chastise***) his fears and anything else that stands in the way of the crown (***golden round***). Fate and the supernatural (***metaphysical aid***) seem on his side. *Do you think Lady Macbeth is right about her husband?*

39 *had the speed of him:* rode faster than he.

dearest partner of greatness, that thou mightst not lose
the dues of rejoicing by being ignorant of what
greatness is promised thee. Lay it to thy heart, and
farewell."
15 Glamis thou art, and Cawdor, and shalt be
What thou art promised. Yet do I fear thy nature.
It is too full o' the milk of human kindness
To catch the nearest way. Thou wouldst be great;
Art not without ambition, but without
20 The illness should attend it. What thou wouldst highly,
That wouldst thou holily; wouldst not play false,
And yet wouldst wrongly win. Thou'ldst have, great
        Glamis,
That which cries "Thus thou must do," if thou have it;
25 And that which rather thou dost fear to do
Than wishest should be undone. Hie thee hither,
That I may pour my spirits in thine ear
And chastise with the valor of my tongue
All that impedes thee from the golden round
30 Which fate and metaphysical aid doth seem
To have thee crowned withal.

[Enter Messenger.]

                              What is your tidings?

Messenger. The King comes here tonight.

Lady Macbeth.   Thou'rt mad to say it!
35 Is not thy master with him? who, were't so,
Would have informed for preparation.

Messenger. So please you, it is true. Our Thane is
        coming.
One of my fellows had the speed of him,
40 Who, almost dead for breath, had scarcely more
Than would make up his message.

Lady Macbeth.   Give him tending;
He brings great news.

[Exit Messenger.]

44 **raven:** The harsh cry of the raven, a bird symbolizing evil and misfortune, was supposed to indicate an approaching death.

46-60 Lady Macbeth calls on the spirits of evil to rid her of feminine weakness (**unsex me**) and to block out guilt. She wants no normal pangs of conscience (**compunctious visiting of nature**) to get in the way of her murderous plan. She asks that her mother's milk be turned to bile (**gall**) by the unseen evil forces (**murd'ring ministers, sightless substances**) that exist in nature. Furthermore, she asks that the night wrap (**pall**) itself in darkness as black as hell so that no one may see or stop the crime. *Do you think Lady Macbeth could actually kill Duncan?*

61-62 Lady Macbeth greets her husband, echoing the witches' prophecies.

65 **in the instant:** at this moment.

70-71 **O, never . . . see:** She either wishes that darkness continue to hide her deeds or wishes that Duncan not live through the night.

73-77 **To beguile . . . under't:** To fool (**beguile**) everyone, act as expected at such a time, that is, as a good host. *Who is more like a serpent, Lady Macbeth or her husband?*

The raven himself is hoarse
45 That croaks the fatal entrance of Duncan
Under my battlements. Come, you spirits
That tend on mortal thoughts, unsex me here,
And fill me, from the crown to the toe, top-full
Of direst cruelty! Make thick my blood;
50 Stop up the access and passage to remorse,
That no compunctious visitings of nature
Shake my fell purpose nor keep peace between
The effect and it! Come to my woman's breasts
And take my milk for gall, you murd'ring ministers,
55 Wherever in your sightless substances
You wait on nature's mischief! Come, thick night,
And pall thee in the dunnest smoke of hell,
That my keen knife see not the wound it makes,
Nor heaven peep through the blanket of the dark
60 To cry "Hold, hold!"

[Enter Macbeth.]

Great Glamis! worthy Cawdor!
Greater than both, by the all-hail hereafter!
Thy letters have transported me beyond
This ignorant present, and I feel now
65 The future in the instant.

Macbeth.   My dearest love,
Duncan comes here tonight.

Lady Macbeth.   And when goes hence?

Macbeth. Tomorrow, as he purposes.

70 **Lady Macbeth.**   O, never
Shall sun that morrow see!
Your face, my Thane, is as a book where men
May read strange matters. To beguile the time,
Look like the time; bear welcome in your eye,
75 Your hand, your tongue; look like the innocent
flower,
But be the serpent under't. He that's coming

79 *my dispatch:* my management.

81 *solely sovereign sway:* bring absolute royal power.

84 *To alter . . . fear:* To change your expression (***favor***) is a sign of fear.

Hautboys: oboes.

1 *seat:* location.

4-11 *This guest . . . delicate:* The martin (***martlet***) usually built its nest on a church (***temple***), where every projection (***jutty***), sculptured decoration (***frieze***), support (***buttress***), and convenient corner (***coign of vantage***) offered a good nesting site. Banquo sees the presence of the martin's hanging (***pendent***) nest, a breeding (procreant) place, as a sign of healthy air.

13-16 *The love . . . your trouble:* Even though love can be troublesome, we should be thankful for it. Duncan, knowing that his visit is a great inconvenience, tells Lady Macbeth that it is a sign of love for which she should be thankful.

Must be provided for; and you shall put
This night's great business into my dispatch,
80 Which shall to all our nights and days to come
Give solely sovereign sway and masterdom.

Macbeth. We will speak further.

Lady Macbeth.   Only look up clear.
To alter favor ever is to fear.
85 Leave all the rest to me.

[Exeunt.]

Scene 6 *In front of Macbeth's castle.*

*King Duncan and his party arrive, and Lady
Macbeth welcomes them. Duncan is generous
in his praise of his hosts and eagerly awaits
the arrival of Macbeth.*

[Hautboys and torches. Enter Duncan, Malcolm, Donalbain,
Banquo, Lennox, Macduff, Ross, Angus, *and* Attendants.*]*

Duncan. This castle hath a pleasant seat. The air
Nimbly and sweetly recommends itself
Unto our gentle senses.

Banquo.   This guest of summer,
5 The temple-haunting martlet, does approve
By his loved mansionry that the heaven's breath
Smells wooingly here. No jutty, frieze,
Buttress, nor coign of vantage, but this bird
Hath made his pendent bed and procreant cradle.
10 Where they most breed and haunt, I have observed
The air is delicate.

[Enter Lady Macbeth.*]*

Duncan.   See, see, our honored hostess!
The love that follows us sometime is our trouble,
Which still we thank as love. Herein I teach you
15 How you shall bid God 'ield us for your pains

19 *single business:* weak service. Lady Macbeth claims that nothing she or her husband can do will match Duncan's generosity.

23 *We rest your hermits:* We can only repay you with prayers. The wealthy used to hire hermits to pray for the dead.

25 *coursed him at the heels:* followed him closely.

26 *purveyor:* like a harbinger, one who makes advance arrangements for a royal visit. Duncan says that he wanted to prepare the way for Macbeth.

27 *holp:* helped.

30-33 Legally, Duncan owned everything in his kingdom. Lady Macbeth politely says that they hold his property in trust (*compt*), ready to return it (*make their audit*) whenever he wants. *Why do you think Lady Macbeth is being especially gracious to Duncan?*

And thank us for your trouble.

Lady Macbeth.   All our service
In every point twice done, and then done double,
Were poor and single business to contend
20   Against those honors deep and broad wherewith
Your Majesty loads our house. For those of old,
And the late dignities heaped up to them,
We rest your hermits.

Duncan.   Where's the Thane of Cawdor?
25   We coursed him at the heels and had a purpose
To be his purveyor; but he rides well,
And his great love, sharp as his spur, hath holp him
To his home before us. Fair and noble hostess,
We are your guest tonight.

30   **Lady Macbeth.**   Your servants ever
Have theirs, themselves, and what is theirs, in compt,
To make their audit at your Highness' pleasure,
Still to return your own.

Duncan.   Give me your hand;
35   Conduct me to mine host. We love him highly
And shall continue our graces towards him.
By your leave, hostess.

[Exeunt.]

Scene 7 *A room in Macbeth's castle.*

> *Macbeth has left Duncan in the middle of
> dinner. Alone, he begins to have second
> thoughts about his murderous plan. Lady
> Macbeth enters and discovers that he has
> changed his mind. She scornfully accuses him of
> cowardice and tells him that a true man would
> never back out of a commitment. She reassures
> him of success and explains her plan. She will
> make sure that the king's attendants drink too
> much. When they are fast asleep, Macbeth will
> stab the king with the servants' weapons.*

Sewer: the steward, the servant in charge of arranging the banquet and tasting the King's food; **divers:** different.

1-11 Again, Macbeth argues with himself about murdering the King. If it could be done without causing problems later, then it would be good to do it soon. If Duncan's murder would have no negative consequences and be successfully completed with his death (**surcease**), then Macbeth would risk eternal damnation. He knows, however, that terrible deeds (**Bloody instructions**) often backfire.

12-29 Macbeth reminds himself that he is Duncan's relative, subject, and host and that the King has never abused his royal powers (**faculties**). In fact, Duncan is such a good person that there is no possible reason for his murder except Macbeth's own driving ambition.

[Hautboys. Torches. Enter a Sewer, *and divers* Servants *with dishes and service over the stage. Then enter* Macbeth.]

Macbeth. If it were done when 'tis done, then 'twere well
    It were done quickly. If the assassination
    Could trammel up the consequence, and catch,
5   With his surcease, success, that but this blow
    Might be the be-all and the end-all here,
    But here, upon this bank and shoal of time,
    We'ld jump the life to come. But in these cases
    We still have judgment here, that we but teach
10   Bloody instructions, which, being taught, return
    To plague the inventor. This even-handed justice
    Commends the ingredience of our poisoned chalice
    To our own lips. He's here in double trust:
    First, as I am his kinsman and his subject,
15   Strong both against the deed; then, as his host,
    Who should against his murderer shut the door,
    Not bear the knife myself. Besides, this Duncan
    Hath borne his faculties so meek, hath been
    So clear in his great office, that his virtues
20   Will plead like angels, trumpet-tongued, against
    The deep damnation of his taking-off;
    And pity, like a naked new-born babe,
    Striding the blast, or heaven's cherubin, horsed
    Upon the sightless couriers of the air,
25   Shall blow the horrid deed in every eye,
    That tears shall drown the wind. I have no spur
    To prick the sides of my intent, but only
    Vaulting ambition, which o'erleaps itself
    And falls on the other—

[Enter Lady Macbeth.]

30   How now? What news?

Lady Macbeth. He has almost supped. Why have you left the chamber?

36-39 *I have . . . so soon:* The praises that Macbeth has received are, like new clothes, to be worn, not quickly thrown away. *What has Macbeth decided?*

40-43 *Was the hope drunk . . . freely:* Lady Macbeth sarcastically describes Macbeth's ambition to be king (*hope*) in drinking terms. His ambition must have been drunk, because it now seems to have a hangover (*to look so green and pale*).

44-50 *Such I . . . adage:* Lady Macbeth criticizes Macbeth's weakened resolve to secure the crown (*ornament of life*) and calls him a coward. She compares him to a cat in a proverb (*adage*) who wouldn't catch fish because it feared wet feet.

51 *Prithee:* a short form of "pray thee," meaning "please."

55 *enterprise:* promise.
56 *durst:* dared.

58-62 *Nor time . . . unmake you:* You talked bravely when the time was not right to act. Now that we have the opportunity (*fitness*), you are afraid.

62 *I have given suck:* I have nursed a baby.

Macbeth. Hath he asked for me?

Lady Macbeth.   Know you not he has?

35 **Macbeth.** We will proceed no further in this business.
　　He hath honored me of late, and I have bought
　　Golden opinions from all sorts of people,
　　Which would be worn now in their newest gloss,
　　Not cast aside so soon.

40 **Lady Macbeth.**   Was the hope drunk
　　Wherein you dressed yourself? Hath it slept since?
　　And wakes it now to look so green and pale
　　At what it did so freely? From this time
　　Such I account thy love. Art thou afeard
45　To be the same in thine own act and valor
　　As thou art in desire? Wouldst thou have that
　　Which thou esteem'st the ornament of life,
　　And live a coward in thine own esteem,
　　Letting "I dare not" wait upon "I would,"
50　Like the poor cat i' the adage?

Macbeth.   Prithee peace!
　　I dare do all that may become a man.
　　Who dares do more is none.

Lady Macbeth.   What beast was't then
55　That made you break this enterprise to me?
　　When you durst do it, then you were a man;
　　And to be more than what you were, you would
　　Be so much more the man. Nor time nor place
　　Did then adhere, and yet you would make both.
60　They have made themselves, and that their fitness
　　　now
　　Does unmake you. I have given suck, and know
　　How tender 'tis to love the babe that milks me.
　　I would, while it was smiling in my face,
65　Have plucked my nipple from his boneless gums
　　And dashed the brains out, had I so sworn as you
　　Have done to this.

70 ***But . . . place:*** When each string of a guitar or lute is tightened to the peg (***sticking place***), the instrument is ready to be played.

73 ***chamberlains:*** servants; attendants.

74 ***wassail:*** carousing; partying.

75-77 ***That memory . . . A limbeck only:*** Memory was thought to be at the base of the brain, where it guarded against harmful vapors rising from the body. Lady Macbeth will get the guards so drunk that their memories will become confused and their reason will become like a still (***limbeck***) producing confused thoughts.

81 ***spongy:*** drunken.

82 ***quell:*** murder.

83-85 ***Bring forth . . . males:*** Your bold spirit (***undaunted mettle***) is better suited to raising males than females. *Do you think Macbeth's words express admiration?*

85 ***received:*** believed.

92-95 ***I am settled . . . know:*** Now that Macbeth has made up his mind, every part of his body (***each corporal agent***) is tightened like a bow. He and Lady Macbeth will return to the banquet and deceive everyone (***mock the time***), hiding their evil intent with gracious faces.

Macbeth.   If we should fail?

Lady Macbeth.   We fail?
70   But screw your courage to the sticking place,
     And we'll not fail. When Duncan is asleep
     (Whereto the rather shall his day's hard journey
     Soundly invite him), his two chamberlains
     Will I with wine and wassail so convince
75   That memory, the warder of the brain,
     Shall be a fume, and the receipt of reason
     A limbeck only. When in swinish sleep
     Their drenched natures lie as in a death,
     What cannot you and I perform upon
80   The unguarded Duncan? what not put upon
     His spongy officers, who shall bear the guilt
     Of our great quell?

Macbeth.   Bring forth men-children only,
     For thy undaunted mettle should compose
85   Nothing but males. Will it not be received,
     When we have marked with blood those sleepy two
     Of his own chamber and used their very daggers,
     That they have done't?

Lady Macbeth.   Who dares receive it other,
90   As we shall make our griefs and clamor roar
     Upon his death?

Macbeth.   I am settled and bend up
     Each corporal agent to this terrible feat.
     Away, and mock the time with fairest show;
95   False face must hide what the false heart doth know.

[Exeunt.]

5-7 ***husbandry . . . candles are all out:*** The heavens show economy (***husbandry***) by keeping the lights (***candles***) out—it is a starless night.

7 ***that:*** perhaps his sword belt or dagger.

8 ***heavy summons:*** desire for sleep.

9-11 ***Merciful powers . . . repose:*** Banquo prays to angels (***merciful powers***) to help him combat bad dreams (***cursed thoughts***).

ACT TWO

Scene 1 *The court of Macbeth's castle.*

> It is past midnight, and Banquo and his son
> Fleance cannot sleep. When Macbeth appears,
> Banquo tells of his uneasy dreams about the
> witches. Macbeth promises that they will
> discuss the prophecies later, and Banquo goes
> to bed. Once alone, Macbeth imagines a
> dagger leading him toward the king's
> chamber. When he hears a bell, the signal
> from Lady Macbeth, he knows it is time to go
> to Duncan's room.

[Enter Banquo, *and* Fleance *with a torch before him.]*

Banquo. How goes the night, boy?

Fleance. The moon is down; I have not heard the clock.

Banquo. And she goes down at twelve.

Fleance.   I take't, 'tis later,
    sir.

5 **Banquo.** Hold, take my sword. There's husbandry in
        heaven;
    Their candles are all out. Take thee that too.
    A heavy summons lies like lead upon me,
    And yet I would not sleep. Merciful powers,
10   Restrain in me the cursed thoughts that nature
    Gives way to in repose!

[Enter Macbeth, *and a* Servant *with a torch.]*

                                Give me my sword.
    Who's there?

17 *largess to your offices:* gifts to the servants' quarters.

18 *withal:* with.

19 *shut up:* went to bed.

21-23 *Being . . . wrought:* Because we were unprepared, we could not entertain the King as we would have liked. *Do you believe in Macbeth's sincerity here?*

28 *can entreat an hour:* both have the time.

32-37 *If you . . . be counseled:* Macbeth asks Banquo for his support (***cleave to my consent***), promising honors in return. Banquo is willing to increase (***augment***) his honor provided he can keep a clear conscience and remain loyal to the King (***keep / My bosom . . . clear***). *How do you think Macbeth feels about Banquo's virtuous stand?*

42-52 *Is this a dagger . . . to use:* Macbeth sees a dagger hanging in midair before him and questions whether it is real (***palpable***) or the illusion of a disturbed (***heat-oppressed***) mind. The floating, imaginary dagger, which leads (***marshal'st***) him to Duncan's room, prompts him to draw his own dagger. *Is Macbeth losing his mind?*

Macbeth. A friend.

15 **Banquo.** What, sir, not yet at rest? The King's abed.
He hath been in unusual pleasure and
Sent forth great largess to your offices.
This diamond he greets your wife withal
By the name of most kind hostess, and shut up
20 In measureless content.

Macbeth.   Being unprepared,
Our will became the servant to defect,
Which else should free have wrought.

Banquo.   All's well.
25 I dreamt last night of the three Weird Sisters.
To you they have showed some truth.

Macbeth.   I think not of them.
Yet when we can entreat an hour to serve,
We would spend it in some words upon that business,
30 If you would grant the time.

Banquo.   At your kind'st leisure.

Macbeth. If you shall cleave to my consent, when 'tis,
It shall make honor for you.

Banquo.   So I lose none
35 In seeking to augment it but still keep
My bosom franchised and allegiance clear,
I shall be counseled.

Macbeth.   Good repose the while!

Banquo. Thanks, sir. The like to you!

[Exeunt Banquo *and* Fleance.*]*

40 **Macbeth.** Go bid thy mistress, when my drink is ready,
She strike upon the bell. Get thee to bed.

[Exit Servant.*]*

Is this a dagger which I see before me,

53-54 *Mine eyes . . . the rest:* Either his eyes are mistaken (*fools*) or his other senses are.

55 *on thy blade . . . blood:* drops of blood on the blade and handle.

60-65 *Witchcraft . . . ghost:* The acts of witches and other evil creatures please Hecate, goddess of the night and witchcraft. Macbeth compares murder to a ghost who steals through the night like Tarquin, an ancient Roman who attacked a sleeping maiden.

67 *prate of:* talk of or reveal.

69-70 *Whiles I . . . gives:* Talk (*threat*) delays action (*deeds*).

72 *knell:* funeral bell.

The handle toward my hand? Come, let me clutch thee!
I have thee not, and yet I see thee still.
45 Art thou not, fatal vision, sensible
To feeling as to sight? or art thou but
A dagger of the mind, a false creation,
Proceeding from the heat-oppressed brain?
I see thee yet, in form as palpable
50 As this which now I draw.
Thou marshal'st me the way that I was going,
And such an instrument I was to use.
Mine eyes are made the fools o' the other senses,
Or else worth all the rest. I see thee still;
55 And on thy blade and dudgeon gouts of blood,
Which was not so before. There's no such thing.
It is the bloody business which informs
Thus to mine eyes. Now o'er the one half-world
Nature seems dead, and wicked dreams abuse
60 The curtained sleep. Witchcraft celebrates
Pale Hecate's offerings; and withered murder,
Alarumed by his sentinel, the wolf,
Whose howl's his watch, thus with his stealthy pace,
With Tarquin's ravishing strides, towards his design
65 Moves like a ghost. Thou sure and firm-set earth,
Hear not my steps which way they walk, for fear
Thy very stones prate of my whereabout
And take the present horror from the time,
Which now suits with it. Whiles I threat, he lives;
70 Words to the heat of deeds too cold breath gives.

[A bell rings.]

I go, and it is done. The bell invites me.
Hear it not, Duncan, for it is a knell
That summons thee to heaven, or to hell.

[Exit.]

5 ***fatal bellman:*** town crier.

7 ***surfeited grooms:*** drunken servants.

9 ***possets:*** drinks.

13-14 *Why does the sound of Macbeth's voice make his wife so afraid?*

15 ***confounds:*** destroys. If Duncan survives, they will be killed (as his attempted murderers).

Scene 2 *Macbeth's castle.*

As Lady Macbeth waits for her husband, she explains how she drugged Duncan's servants. Suddenly a dazed and terrified Macbeth enters, carrying the bloody daggers that he used to murder Duncan. He imagines a voice that warns, "Macbeth shall sleep no more" and is too afraid to return to the scene of the crime. Lady Macbeth takes the bloody daggers back so that the servants will be blamed. Startled by a knocking at the gate, she hurries back and tells Macbeth to wash off the blood and change into his nightclothes.

[Enter Lady Macbeth.*]*

Lady Macbeth. That which hath made them drunk
    hath made me bold;
    What hath quenched them hath given me fire. Hark!
    Peace!
5   It was the owl that shrieked, the fatal bellman
    Which gives the stern'st good-night. He is about it.
    The doors are open, and the surfeited grooms
    Do mock their charge with snores. I have drugged
    their possets,
10   That death and nature do contend about them
    Whether they live or die.

Macbeth. *[Within]* Who's there? What, ho?

Lady Macbeth. Alack, I am afraid they have awaked,
    And 'tis not done! The attempt, and not the deed,
15   Confounds us. Hark! I laid their daggers ready;
    He could not miss 'em. Had he not resembled
    My father as he slept, I had done't.

[Enter Macbeth.*]*

                      My husband!

Macbeth. I have done the deed. Didst thou not hear a
20   noise?

33 A troubled Macbeth begins his descriptions of the voices he heard in the castle.

42-43 *As they . . . fear:* He imagines that the sleepers could see him listening to their exclamations of fear, with his hands bloody like those of an executioner.

43-48 *Why is Macbeth so troubled by the fact that he cannot say "Amen"?*

Lady Macbeth. I heard the owl scream and the crickets cry.
Did not you speak?

Macbeth.　　　　　　When?

25　**Lady Macbeth.**　　　　　　Now.

Macbeth.　　　　　　　　　As I descended?

Lady Macbeth. Ay.

Macbeth. Hark!
Who lies i' the second chamber?

30　**Lady Macbeth.**　　　　　　Donalbain.

Macbeth. This is a sorry sight.

Lady Macbeth. A foolish thought, to say a sorry sight.

Macbeth. There's one did laugh in's sleep, and one cried "Murder!"
35　That they did wake each other. I stood and heard them.
But they did say their prayers and addressed them
Again to sleep.

Lady Macbeth. There are two lodged together.

40　**Macbeth.** One cried "God bless us!" and "Amen!" the other,
As they had seen me with these hangman's hands,
List'ning their fear. I could not say "Amen!"
When they did say "God bless us!"

45　**Lady Macbeth.** Consider it not so deeply.

Macbeth. But wherefore could not I pronounce "Amen"?
I had most need of blessing, and "Amen"
Stuck in my throat.

Lady Macbeth.　　　　　These deeds must not be thought
50　After these ways. So, it will make us mad.

52-56 *the innocent sleep . . . life's feast:* Sleep eases
worries (*knits up the raveled sleave of care*),
relieves the aches of physical work (*sore labor's bath*),
soothes the anxious (*hurt minds*), and nourishes like
food. *Why is Macbeth so concerned about sleep?*

65 *this filthy witness:* the evidence, that is, the blood.

72 *Infirm of purpose:* weak-willed.

74-75 *'Tis . . . a painted devil:* She compares his fears to
those that children have of a devil's picture (*painted
devil*).

76-77 *I'll gild . . . guilt:* She'll cover (*gild*) the servants with
blood, blaming them for the murder. *How is her
attitude toward blood different from her husband's?*

80 *they pluck out mine eyes:* In the Bible, Jesus tells his
followers that if their eyes cause them to do evil, they
should pluck them out.

82-84 *This my hand . . . one red:* The blood on my hand
will redden (*incarnadine*) the seas.

Macbeth. Methought I heard a voice cry "Sleep no more!
    Macbeth does murder sleep"—the innocent sleep,
    Sleep that knits up the raveled sleave of care,
    The death of each day's life, sore labor's bath,
55   Balm of hurt minds, great nature's second course,
    Chief nourisher in life's feast.

Lady Macbeth.   What do you mean?

Macbeth. Still it cried "Sleep no more!" to all the house;
    "Glamis hath murdered sleep, and therefore Cawdor
60   Shall sleep no more! Macbeth shall sleep no more!"

Lady Macbeth. Who was it that thus cried? Why, worthy
    Thane,
    You do unbend your noble strength to think
    So brainsickly of things. Go get some water
65   And wash this filthy witness from your hand.
    Why did you bring these daggers from the place?
    They must lie there. Go carry them and smear
    The sleepy grooms with blood.

Macbeth.   I'll go no more.
70   I am afraid to think what I have done;
    Look on't again I dare not.

Lady Macbeth.   Infirm of purpose!
    Give me the daggers. The sleeping and the dead
    Are but as pictures. 'Tis the eye of childhood
75   That fears a painted devil. If he do bleed,
    I'll gild the faces of the grooms withal,
    For it must seem their guilt. *[Exit. Knocking within.]*

Macbeth.   Whence is that knocking?
    How is't with me when every noise appals me?
80   What hands are here? Ha! they pluck out mine eyes!
    Will all great Neptune's ocean wash this blood
    Clean from my hand? No. This my hand will rather
    The multitudinous seas incarnadine,
    Making the green one red.

[Enter Lady Macbeth.*]*

89-90 *Your constancy . . . unattended:* Your courage has left you.

92-93 *lest . . . watchers:* in case we are called for and found awake (***watchers***), which would look suspicious.

95 *To know . . . myself:* To come to terms with what I have done, I must forget about my conscience.

2 *old turning the key:* plenty of key turning. Hell's porter would be busy because so many people are ending up in hell these days.

4 *Belzebub:* a devil.

4-19 The porter pretends he is welcoming a farmer who killed himself after his schemes to get rich (***expectation of plenty***) failed, a double talker (***equivocator***) who perjured himself yet couldn't talk his way into heaven, and a tailor who cheated his customers by skimping on material (***stealing out of a French hose***). The tailor will now get plenty of heat for his iron (***roast your goose***). Tradition holds that hell is populated with people who took the easy way (***primrose way***) in life.

85 **Lady Macbeth.** My hands are of your color, but I shame
To wear a heart so white. *[Knock.]* I hear a knocking
At the south entry. Retire we to our chamber.
A little water clears us of this deed.
How easy is it then! Your constancy
90 Hath left you unattended. *[Knock.]* Hark! more
knocking.
Get on your nightgown, lest occasion call us
And show us to be watchers. Be not lost
So poorly in your thoughts.

95 **Macbeth.** To know my deed, 'twere best not know myself.

[Knock.]

Wake Duncan with thy knocking! I would thou couldst!

[Exeunt.]

Scene 3 *Within Macbeth's castle, near the gate.*

*The drunken porter staggers across the
courtyard to answer the knocking. After Lennox
and Macduff are let in, Macbeth arrives to lead
them to the king's quarters. Macduff enters
Duncan's room and discovers his murder. Lennox
and Macbeth then go to the scene, and
Macbeth, pretending to be enraged, kills the
two servants. Amid all the commotion, Lady
Macbeth faints. Duncan's sons, Malcolm and
Donalbain, fearing for their lives, quietly leave,
hoping to escape the country.*

[Enter a Porter. *Knocking within.]*

Porter. Here's a knocking indeed! If a man were porter
of hell gate, he should have old turning the key.
[Knock.] Knock, knock, knock! Who's there, i' the name
of Belzebub? Here's a farmer that hanged himself on
5 the expectation of plenty. Come in time! Have napkins
enow about you; here you'll sweat for't. *(Knock.)*

19 *Anon:* soon.

19-20 *I pray . . . the porter:* He wants a tip.

23 *second cock:* early morning, announced by the crow of a rooster.

27 *nose-painting:* the reddening of the nose from heavy drinking.

28-35 The porter jokes that alcohol stimulates lust (*Lechery*) but makes the lover a failure. When drunk, the lover cannot stand up to (*stand to*) the demands of love and instead falls asleep.

36-40 More jokes about alcohol, this time described as a wrestler finally thrown off (*cast*) by the porter, who thus paid him back (*requited him*) for disappointment in love. *Cast* also means "to vomit" or "to urinate," two other ways of dealing with alcohol.

Knock, knock! Who's there, in the other devil's name?
Faith, here's an equivocator, that could swear in both
the scales against either scale; who committed treason
enough for God's sake, yet could not equivocate to
heaven. O, come in, equivocator! *[Knock.]* Knock,
knock, knock! Who's there? Faith, here's an English
tailor come hither for stealing out of a French hose.
Come in, tailor. Here you may roast your goose.
[Knock.] Knock, knock! Never at quiet! What are you?
But this place is too cold for hell. I'll devilporter it no
further. I had thought to have let in some of all
professions that go the primrose way to the everlasting
bonfire. *[Knock.]* Anon, anon! *[Opens the gate.]* I pray
you remember the porter.

[Enter Macduff and Lennox.]

Macduff. Was it so late, friend, ere you went to bed,
That you do lie so late?

Porter. Faith, sir, we were carousing till the second cock;
and drink, sir, is a great provoker of three things.

Macduff. What three things does drink especially
provoke?

Porter. Marry, sir, nose-painting, sleep, and urine.
Lechery, sir, it provokes, and unprovokes: it provokes
the desire, but it takes away the performance.
Therefore much drink may be said to be an
equivocator with lechery: it makes him, and it mars
him; it sets him on, and it takes him off; it persuades
him, and disheartens him; makes him stand to, and not
stand to; in conclusion, equivocates him in a sleep, and,
giving him the lie, leaves him.

Macduff. I believe drink gave thee the lie last night.

Porter. That it did, sir, i' the very throat on me; but I
requited him for his lie; and, I think, being too strong
for him, though he took up my legs sometime, yet I
made a shift to cast him.

47 *timely:* early.

48 *slipped the hour:* missed the time.

52 *physics:* cures.

55 *limited service:* appointed duty.

58-65 Lennox discusses the strange events of the night, from fierce winds to the continuous shrieking (***strange screams of death***) of an owl (***obscure bird***). The owl's scream, a sign of death, bodes more (***New hatched***) uproar (***combustion***) and confusion.

67-68 I cannot remember another night as bad as this.

Macduff. Is thy master stirring?

[Enter Macbeth.]

    Our knocking has awaked him; here he comes.

Lennox. Good morrow, noble sir.

Macbeth.   Good morrow, both.

45 **Macduff.** Is the King stirring, worthy Thane?

Macbeth.   Not yet.

Macduff. He did command me to call timely on him;
I have almost slipped the hour.

Macbeth.   I'll bring you to him.

50 **Macduff.** I know this is a joyful trouble to you;
But yet 'tis one.

Macbeth. The labor we delight in physics pain.
This is the door.

Macduff.   I'll make so bold to call,
55 For 'tis my limited service. *[Exit.]*

Lennox. Goes the King hence today?

Macbeth.   He does; he did appoint so.

Lennox. The night has been unruly. Where we lay,
Our chimneys were blown down, and, as they say,
60 Lamentings heard i' the air, strange screams of death,
And prophesying, with accents terrible,
Of dire combustion and confused events
New hatched to the woeful time. The obscure bird
Clamored the livelong night. Some say the earth
65 was feverous and did shake.

Macbeth.   'Twas a rough night.

Lennox. My young remembrance cannot parallel
A fellow to it.

72-75 Macduff mourns Duncan's death as the destruction (**Confusion**) of order and as (**sacrilegious**), violating all that is holy. In Shakespeare's time the king was believed to be God's sacred representative on earth.

79 *new Gorgon:* Macduff compares the shocking sight of the corpse to a Gorgon, a monster of Greek mythology with snakes for hair. Anyone who saw a Gorgon turned to stone.

84 *counterfeit:* imitation.

86 *great doom's image:* a picture like the Last Judgment, the end of the world.

87 *sprites:* spirits. The spirits of the dead were supposed to rise on Judgment Day.

90 *trumpet calls to parley:* She compares the clanging bell to a trumpet used to call two sides of a battle to negotiation.

[Enter Macduff.]

Macduff. O horror, horror, horror! Tongue nor heart
70   Cannot conceive nor name thee!

Macbeth and Lennox.   What's the matter?

Macduff. Confusion now hath made his masterpiece!
     Most sacrilegious murder hath broke ope
     The Lord's anointed temple and stole thence
75   The life o' the building!

Macbeth.   What is't you say? the life?

Lennox. Mean you his majesty?

Macduff. Approach the chamber, and destroy your sight
     With a new Gorgon. Do not bid me speak.
80   See, and then speak yourselves.

[Exeunt Macbeth and Lennox.]

                 Awake, awake!
     Ring the alarum bell. Murder and treason!
     Banquo and Donalbain! Malcolm! awake!
     Shake off this downy sleep, death's counterfeit,
85   And look on death itself! Up, up, and see
     The great doom's image! Malcolm! Banquo!
     As from your graves rise up and walk like sprites
     To countenance this horror! Ring the bell!

[Bell rings.]

[Enter Lady Macbeth.]

Lady Macbeth. What's the business,
90   That such a hideous trumpet calls to parley
     The sleepers of the house? Speak, speak!

Macduff.   O gentle lady,
     'Tis not for you to hear what I can speak!
     The repetition in a woman's ear
95   Would murder as it fell.

[Enter Banquo.]

104-108 *for from . . . brag of:* From now on, nothing matters (*There's nothing serious*) in human life (*mortality*); even fame and grace have been made meaningless. The good wine of life has been removed (*drawn*), leaving only the dregs (*lees*). *Is Macbeth being completely insincere, or does he regret his crime?*

116 *badged:* marked.

O Banquo, Banquo,
Our royal master's murdered!

Lady Macbeth.   Woe, alas!
What, in our house?

100 **Banquo.**   Too cruel anywhere.
Dear Duff, I prithee contradict thyself
And say it is not so.

[Enter Macbeth, Lennox, and Ross.]

Macbeth. Had I but died an hour before this chance,
I had lived a blessed time; for from this instant
105 There's nothing serious in mortality;
All is but toys; renown and grace is dead;
The wine of life is drawn, and the mere lees
Is left this vault to brag of.

[Enter Malcolm and Donalbain.]

Donalbain. What is amiss?

110 **Macbeth.**   You are, and do not know't.
The spring, the head, the fountain of your blood
Is stopped, the very source of it is stopped.

Macduff. Your royal father's murdered.

Malcolm.   O, by whom?

115 **Lennox.** Those of his chamber, as it seemed, had done't.
Their hands and faces were all badged with blood;
So were their daggers, which unwiped we found
Upon their pillows.
They stared and were distracted. No man's life
120 Was to be trusted with them.

Macbeth. O, yet I do repent me of my fury
That I did kill them.

Macduff.   Wherefore did you so?

Macbeth. Who can be wise, amazed, temp'rate, and
125 furious,

127-128. *The . . . reason:* He claims his emotions overpowered his reason, which would have made him pause to think before he killed Duncan's servants.

130 *breach:* a military term to describe a break in defenses, such as a hole in a castle wall.

132-133 *their daggers . . . gore:* their knives shamefully clothed in blood.

136 Lady Macbeth faints. *Is she only pretending?*

138-140 *Why do . . . ours:* Malcolm wonders why he and Donalbain are silent since they have the most right to discuss the topic (*argument*) of their father's death.

141-145 Donalbain fears that a treacherous fate may await them at Macbeth's castle; destruction may lurk anywhere, as if concealed in a small hole.

146-147 Our deep sorrow has not yet moved us to action.

149-152 Banquo suggests that they all meet to discuss the murder after they have dressed (*our naked frailities hid*), since people are shivering in their nightclothes (*suffer in exposure*).

152-155 Though shaken by fears and doubts (*scruples*), he will fight against the secret plans (*undivulged pretense*) of the traitor. *Do you think Banquo suspects Macbeth?*

Loyal and neutral, in a moment? No man.
The expedition of my violent love
Outrun the pauser, reason. Here lay Duncan,
His silver skin laced with his golden blood,
130   And his gashed stabs looked like a breach in nature
For ruin's wasteful entrance; there, the murderers,
Steeped in the colors of their trade, their daggers
Unmannerly breeched with gore. Who could refrain
That had a heart to love and in that heart
135   Courage to make's love known?

Lady Macbeth.   Help me hence, ho!

Macduff. Look to the lady.

Malcolm. *[Aside to* Donalbain*]* Why do we hold our
        tongues,
140   That most may claim this argument for ours?

Donalbain. *[Aside to* Malcolm*]* What should be spoken
        here,
Where our fate, hid in an auger hole,
May rush and seize us? Let's away,
145   Our tears are not yet brewed.

Malcolm. *[Aside to* Donalbain*]* Nor our strong sorrow
Upon the foot of motion.

Banquo.   Look to the lady.

*[*Lady Macbeth *is carried out.]*

And when we have our naked frailties hid,
150   That suffer in exposure, let us meet
And question this most bloody piece of work,
To know it further. Fears and scruples shake us.
In the great hand of God I stand, and thence
Against the undivulged pretense I fight
155   Of treasonous malice.

Macduff.   And so do I.

All.   So all.

161-163 Malcolm does not want to join (***consort with***) the others because one of them may have plotted the murder.

166-167 ***the near . . . bloody:*** Being Duncan's sons, they are in greatest danger of more bloodshed.

168-170 ***This . . . avoid the aim:*** Malcolm uses an archery metaphor to express his fear of assassination. The arrow (***shaft***) has not yet hit its target.

172-173 ***There's . . . left:*** There's good reason (***warrant***) to steal away from a situation that promises no mercy.

1-4 Nothing the old man has seen in seventy years (***Threescore and ten***) has been as strange and terrible (***sore***) as this night. It has made other times seem trivial (***hath trifled***) by comparison.

Macbeth. Let's briefly put on manly readiness
  And meet i' the hall together.

All.   Well contented.

[Exeunt all but Malcolm *and* Donalbain.*]*

Malcolm. What will you do? Let's not consort with them.
  To show an unfelt sorrow is an office
  Which the false man does easy. I'll to England.

Donalbain. To Ireland I. Our separated fortune
165 Shall keep us both the safer. Where we are,
  There's daggers in men's smiles; the near in blood,
  The nearer bloody.

Malcolm.   This murderous shaft that's shot
  Hath not yet lighted, and our safest way
170 Is to avoid the aim. Therefore to horse!
  And let us not be dainty of leave-taking
  But shift away. There's warrant in that theft
  Which steals itself when there's no mercy left.

[Exeunt.]

Scene 4 *Outside Macbeth's castle.*

*Ross and an old man discuss recent unnatural
events, including the strange darkness of the
day and news that the king's horses have eaten
each other. Macduff enters and tells them that
Duncan's sons, who have fled, are accused of
plotting his murder. Macbeth has been named
king and will soon be crowned. Ross plans to
attend the ceremony, but Macduff, uneasy with
what has occurred, decides to return home.*

[Enter Ross *with an* Old Man.*]*

Old Man. Threescore and ten I can remember well;
  Within the volume of which time I have seen
  Hours dreadful and things strange; but this sore night
  Hath trifled former knowings.

6 *as:* as if.

7 *stage:* world.

8-11 *And yet . . . kiss it:* Though daytime, an unnatural darkness blots out the sun (*strangles the traveling lamp*).

14-15 *A falcon . . . and killed:* The owl would never be expected to attack a highflying (*tow'ring*) falcon, much less defeat one. Such an act is a sure sign of nature's disruption.

18 *minions:* best or favorites.

20 *Contending 'gainst obedience:* The well-trained horses rebelliously fought against all contraints.

31 He wonders what the servants could have hoped to achieve (*pretend*) by killing.

32 *suborned:* hired or bribed.

Ross.   Ah, good father,
5   Thou seest the heavens, as troubled with man's act,
    Threaten his bloody stage. By the clock 'tis day,
    And yet dark night strangles the traveling lamp.
    Is't night's predominance, or the day's shame,
10 That darkness does the face of earth entomb
    When living light should kiss it?

Old Man.   'Tis unnatural,
    Even like the deed that's done. On Tuesday last
    A falcon, tow'ring in her pride of place,
15 Was by a mousing owl hawked at and killed.

Ross. And Duncan's horses (a thing most strange and
        certain),
    Beauteous and swift, the minions of their race,
    Turned wild in nature, broke their stalls, flung out,
20 Contending 'gainst obedience, as they would make
    War with mankind.

Old Man.   'Tis said they eat each other.

Ross. They did so, to the amazement of mine eyes
    That looked upon't.

[Enter Macduff.]

25   Here comes the good Macduff.
    How goes the world, sir, now?

Macduff.   Why, see you not?

Ross. Is't known who did this more than bloody deed?

Macduff. Those that Macbeth hath slain.

30 **Ross.**   Alas, the day!
    What good could they pretend?

Macduff.   They were suborned.
    Malcolm and Donalbain, the King's two sons,
    Are stol'n away and fled, which puts upon them
35 Suspicion of the deed.

36-38 He is horrified by the thought that the sons could act contrary to nature (*'Gainst nature still*) because of wasteful (*Thriftless*) ambition and greedily destroy (*raven up*) their father, the source of their own life (*Thine own live's means*).

40-41 *to Scone . . . invested:* Macbeth went to the traditional site (*Scone*) where Scotland's kings were crowned.

51 *Lest our . . . new:* He fears that life under Macbeth's rule might be harsher than under Duncan (*our old robes*).

53-54 The old man give his blessing (*benison*) to Macduff and all those who would restore good and bring peace to the troubled land.

Ross.   'Gainst nature still!
Thriftless ambition, that will raven up
Thine own live's means! Then 'tis most like
The sovereignty will fall upon Macbeth.

40 **Macduff.** He is already named, and gone to Scone
To be invested.

Ross.   Where is Duncan's body?

Macduff. Carried to Colmekill,
The sacred storehouse of his predecessors
45 And guardian of their bones.

Ross.   Will you to Scone?

Macduff. No, cousin, I'll to Fife.

Ross.   Well, I will thither.

Macduff. Well, may you see things well done there.
50   Adieu,
Lest our old robes sit easier than our new!

Ross. Farewell, father.

Old Man. God's benison go with you, and with those
That would make good of bad, and friends of foes!

[Exeunt omnes.]

3-4 *it was said . . . posterity:* It was predicted that the kingship would not remain in your family.

6-10 *If . . . in hope:* Despite Banquo's suspicions of foul play, he is impressed by the truth (*verities*) of the prophecies, which make Macbeth shine with good fortune. He hopes the witches' prediction for him will come true too (*be my oracles as well*).

(*Sennet sounded*)*:* A trumpet is sounded.

ACT THREE

Scene 1 *Macbeth's palace at Forres.*

Banquo voices his suspicions of Macbeth but still hopes that the prophecy about his own children will prove true. Macbeth, as king, enters to request Banquo's presence at a state banquet. Banquo explains that he will be away during the day with his son Fleance but that they will return in time for the banquet. Alone, Macbeth expresses his fear of Banquo, because of the witches' promise that Banquo's sons will be kings. He persuades two murderers to kill Banquo and his son before the banquet.

[Enter Banquo.]

Banquo. Thou hast it now—King, Cawdor, Glamis, all,
As the Weird Women promised; and I fear
Thou play'dst most foully for't. Yet it was said
It should not stand in thy posterity,
5   But that myself should be the root and father
Of many kings. If there come truth from them
(As upon thee, Macbeth, their speeches shine),
Why, by the verities on thee made good,
May they not be my oracles as well
10   And set me up in hope? But, hush, no more!

[Sennet sounded. Enter Macbeth, as King; Lady Macbeth, as Queen; Lennox, Ross, Lords, and Attendants.]

Macbeth. Here's our chief guest.

Lady Macbeth. If he had been forgotten,
It had been as a gap in our great feast,
And all-thing unbecoming.

15-16 When a king speaks, he usually uses the royal pronoun *we*. Notice how Macbeth switches to *I*, keeping a personal tone with Banquo.

17-20 Banquo says he is duty-bound to serve the king. *Do you think his tone is cold or warm here?*

24 *grave and prosperous:* thoughtful and profitable.

28-30 *Go not . . . twain:* If his horse goes no faster than usual, he'll be back an hour or two (*twain*) after dark.

33 *bloody cousins:* murderous relatives (Malcolm and Donalbain); *bestowed:* settled.

35 *parricide:* murder of one's father.

36 *strange invention:* lies; stories they have invented. *What kinds of stories might they be telling?*

37-38 *When . . . jointly:* when matters of state will require the attention of us both.

15 **Macbeth**. Tonight we hold a solemn supper, sir,
And I'll request your presence.

Banquo.   Let your Highness
Command upon me, to the which my duties
Are with a most indissoluble tie
20 For ever knit.

Macbeth.   Ride you this afternoon?

Banquo. Ay, my good lord.

Macbeth. We should have else desired your good advice
(Which still hath been both grave and prosperous)
25 In this day's council; but we'll take tomorrow.
Is't far you ride?

Banquo. As far, my lord, as will fill up the time
'Twixt this and supper. Go not my horse the better,
I must become a borrower of the night
30 For a dark hour or twain.

Macbeth.   Fail not our feast.

Banquo. My lord, I will not.

Macbeth. We hear our bloody cousins are bestowed
In England and in Ireland, not confessing
35 Their cruel parricide, filling their hearers
With strange invention. But of that tomorrow,
When therewithal we shall have cause of state
Craving us jointly. Hie you to horse. Adieu,
Till you return at night. Goes Fleance with you?

40 **Banquo**. Ay, my good lord. Our time does call upon's.

Macbeth. I wish your horses swift and sure of foot,
And so I do commend you to their backs.
Farewell.

[Exit Banquo.*]*

44 *be master of his time:* do what he wants.

47 *While:* until.

48-49 *Sirrah:* a term of address to an inferior; *Attend . . . pleasure:* Are they waiting for me?

52-76 *To be thus . . . safely thus:* To be king is worthless unless my position as king is safe. Macbeth speaks to himself about his fears of Banquo, whose kingly qualities make him a threat.

56 *dauntless temper:* fearless temperament.

60-61 *My . . . Caesar:* Banquo's mere presence seems to force back (*rebuke*) Macbeth's ruling spirit (*genius*). In ancient Rome, Octavius Caesar, who became emperor, had the same effect on his rival, Mark Antony.

61 *chid:* scolded; *Sisters:* the witches.

65-74 They gave me a childless (*fruitless, barren*) crown and scepter, which will be taken away by someone outside my family (*unlineal*). It appears that I have committed murder, poisoned (*filed*) my mind, and destroyed my soul (*eternal jewel*) all for the benefit of Banquo's heirs.

75-76 *Rather . . . utterance:* Rather than allowing Banquo's heirs to become kings, he calls upon Fate itself to enter the combat arena (*list*) so that he can fight it to the death (*utterance*). *Why does he feel that he needs to fight Fate?*

Let every man be master of his time
45   Till seven at night. To make society
The sweeter welcome, we will keep ourself
Till supper time alone. While then, God be with you!

[Exeunt all but Macbeth *and a* Servant.*]*

Sirrah, a word with you. Attend those men
Our pleasure?

50 **Servant.** They are, my lord, without the palace gate.

Macbeth. Bring them before us.

[Exit Servant.*]*

Macbeth.   To be thus is nothing,
But to be safely thus. Our fears in Banquo
Stick deep, and in his royalty of nature
55   Reigns that which would be feared. 'Tis much he dares,
And to that dauntless temper of his mind
He hath a wisdom that doth guide his valor
To act in safety. There is none but he
Whose being I do fear; and under him
60   My genius is rebuked, as it is said
Mark Antony's was by Caesar. He chid the Sisters
When first they put the name of King upon me,
And bade them speak to him. Then, prophet-like,
They hailed him father to a line of kings.
65   Upon my head they placed a fruitless crown
And put a barren scepter in my gripe,
Thence to be wrenched with an unlineal hand,
No son of mine succeeding. If't be so,
For Banquo's issue have I filed my mind;
70   For them the gracious Duncan have I murdered;
Put rancors in the vessel of my peace
Only for them, and mine eternal jewel
Given to the common enemy of man
To make them kings, the seed of Banquo kings!
75   Rather than so, come, Fate, into the list,
And champion me to the utterance! Who's there?

81-90 Macbeth reminds the men of a past conversation in which he argued that Banquo had kept them from good fortune, not he. He supposedly proved (***passed in probation***) Banquo's role, his deception (***How you were borne in hand***), his methods, and his allies. Even a half-wit (***half a soul***) or a crazed person would agree that Banquo caused their trouble.

95-98 He asks whether they are so influenced by the gospel's message of forgiveness (***so gospeled***) that they will pray for Banquo and his children despite his harshness, which will leave their own families beggars.

100-109 Macbeth insults them by saying anyone can be classified as a man, just as anything from a mangy cur to an elegant greyhound goes by the name of dog. The true worth of a dog can only be measured by examining the record (***valued file***) of its special qualities (***particular addition***).

[Enter Servant and two Murderers.]

Now go to the door and stay there till we call.

[Exit Servant.]

Was it not yesterday we spoke together?

Murderers. It was, so please your Highness.

80 **Macbeth.**   Well then, now
Have you considered of my speeches? Know
That it was he, in the times past, which held you
So under fortune, which you thought had been
Our innocent self. This I made good to you
85 In our last conference, passed in probation with you
How you were borne in hand, how crossed; the
        instruments;
Who wrought with them; and all things else that might
To half a soul and to a notion crazed
90 Say "Thus did Banquo."

First Murderer.   You made it known to us.

Macbeth. I did so; and went further, which is now
Our point of second meeting. Do you find
Your patience so predominant in your nature
95 That you can let this go? Are you so gospeled
To pray for this good man and for his issue,
Whose heavy hand hath bowed you to the grave
And beggared yours for ever?

First Murderer.   We are men, my liege.

100 **Macbeth.** Ay, in the catalogue ye go for men,
As hounds and greyhounds, mongrels, spaniels, curs,
Shoughs, water-rugs, and demi-wolves are clept
All by the name of dogs. The valued file
Distinguishes the swift, the slow, the subtle,
105 The housekeeper, the hunter, every one
According to the gift which bounteous nature
Hath in him closed; whereby he does receive

110-116 The men can show their high rank (**station**) only by
agreeing to Macbeth's plan. He will give them a secret
job (**business in your bosoms**) that will earn his
loyalty (**Grapples you to the heart**) and love.
Banquo's death will make this sick king healthy.

119 *incensed:* angered.

122 *tugged with:* knocked about by.

128-130 Banquo is near enough to draw blood, and like a
menacing swordsman, his mere presence threatens
(**thrusts against**) Macbeth's existence.

132 *bid my will avouch it:* justify it as my will.

134 *wail his fall:* I must mourn (**wail**) his death.

136 *do make love:* appeal.

137 *common eye:* public view.

138 *sundry:* various.

Particular addition, from the bill
That writes them all alike; and so of men.
110 Now, if you have a station in the file,
Not i' the worst rank of manhood, say't;
And I will put that business in your bosoms
Whose execution takes your enemy off,
Grapples you to the heart and love of us,
115 Who wear our health but sickly in his life,
Which in his death were perfect.

Second Murderer.   I am one, my liege,
Whom the vile blows and buffets of the world
have so incensed that I am reckless what
120 I do to spite the world.

First Murderer.   And I another,
So weary with disasters, tugged with fortune,
That I would set my life on any chance,
To mend it or be rid on't.

125 **Macbeth.**   Both of you
Know Banquo was your enemy.

Murderers.   True, my lord.

Macbeth. So is he mine, and in such bloody distance
That every minute of his being thrusts
130 Against my near'st of life; and though I could
With barefaced power sweep him from my sight
And bid my will avouch it, yet I must not,
For certain friends that are both his and mine,
Whose loves I may not drop, but wail his fall
135 Who I myself struck down. And thence it is
That I to your assistance do make love,
Masking the business from the common eye
For sundry weighty reasons.

Second Murderer.   We shall, my lord,
140 Perform what you command us.

First Murderer.   Though our lives—

142 *Your spirits shine through you:* Your courage is evident.

147-148 *And something . . . clearness:* The murder must be done away from the palace so that I remain blameless (*I require a clearness*).

151 *absence:* death. *Why is the death of Fleance so important?*

153 *Resolve yourselves apart:* Decide in private.

156 *straight:* soon.

Macbeth. Your spirits shine through you. Within this
    hour at most
I will advise you where to plant yourselves,
145   Acquaint you with the perfect spy o' the time,
The moment on't; for't must be done tonight,
And something from the palace (always thought
That I require a clearness), and with him,
To leave no rubs nor botches in the work,
150   Fleance his son, that keeps him company,
Whose absence is no less material to me
Than is his father's, must embrace the fate
Of that dark hour. Resolve yourselves apart;
I'll come to you anon.

155 **Murderers.**   We are resolved, my lord.

Macbeth. I'll call upon you straight. Abide within.

[Exeunt Murderers.]

It is concluded. Banquo, thy soul's flight,
If it find heaven, must find it out tonight.

[Exit.]

Scene 2 *Macbeth's palace at Forres.*

*Lady Macbeth and her husband discuss the
troubled thoughts and bad dreams they have
had since Duncan's murder. However, they agree
to hide their dark emotions at the night's
banquet. Lady Macbeth tries to comfort the
tormented Macbeth, but her words do no good.
Instead, Macbeth hints at some terrible event
that will occur that night.*

[Enter Lady Macbeth and a Servant.]

Lady Macbeth. Is Banquo gone from court?

Servant. Ay, madam, but returns again tonight.

6-9 Nothing (**Naught**) has been gained; everything has been wasted (**spent**). It would be better to be dead like Duncan than to live in uncertain joy.

10-14 *Does Lady Macbeth follow her own advice about forgetting Duncan's murder?*

18-25 He would rather have the world fall apart (**the frame of things disjoint**) than be afflicted with such fears and nightmares. Death is preferable to life on the torture rack of mental anguish (**restless ecstasy**).

31 *sleek:* smooth.

Lady Macbeth. Say to the King I would attend his leisure
For a few words.

5 **Servant.**   Madam, I will.

[Exit.]

Lady Macbeth.   Naught's had, all's spent,
Where our desire is got without content.
'Tis safer to be that which we destroy
Than by destruction dwell in doubtful joy.

[Enter Macbeth.]

10 How now, my lord? Why do you keep alone,
Of sorriest fancies your companions making,
Using those thoughts which should indeed have died
With them they think on? Things without all remedy
Should be without regard. What's done is done.

15 **Macbeth.** We have scotched the snake, not killed it.
She'll close and be herself, whilst our poor malice
Remains in danger of her former tooth.
But let the frame of things disjoint, both the worlds
    suffer,
20 Ere we will eat our meal in fear and sleep
In the affliction of these terrible dreams
That shake us nightly. Better be with the dead,
Whom we, to gain our peace, have sent to peace,
Than on the torture of the mind to lie
25 In restless ecstasy. Duncan is in his grave;
After life's fitful fever he sleeps well.
Treason has done his worst: nor steel nor poison,
Malice domestic, foreign levy, nothing,
Can touch him further.

30 **Lady Macbeth.**   Come on.
Gentle my lord, sleek o'er your rugged looks;
Be bright and jovial among your guests tonight.

Macbeth. So shall I, love; and so, I pray, be you.
Let your remembrance apply to Banquo;

35 *Present him eminence:* Pay special attention to him.

37 *lave . . . streams:* wash (*lave*) our honor in streams of flattery, that is, falsify our feelings.

38 *vizards:* masks.

43 *in them . . . not eterne:* Nature did not give them immortality.

45-49 *jocund:* cheerful; merry; *Ere the bat . . . note:* Before nightfall, when the bats and beetles fly, something dreadful will happen.

51 *chuck:* chick, a term of affection.

52 *seeling:* blinding.

55 *great bond:* Banquo's life.

56 *thickens:* darkens.

57 *rooky:* gloomy; also, filled with crows (rooks).

61 Things brought about through evil need additional evil to make them strong.

35 Present him eminence both with eye and tongue:
Unsafe the while, that we
Must lave our honors in these flattering streams
And make our faces vizards to our hearts,
Disguising what they are.

40 **Lady Macbeth.** You must leave this.

Macbeth. O, full of scorpions is my mind, dear wife!
Thou know'st that Banquo, and his Fleance, lives.

Lady Macbeth. But in them Nature's copy's not eterne.

Macbeth. There's comfort yet; they are assailable.
45 Then be thou jocund. Ere the bat hath flown
His cloistered flight, ere to black Hecate's summons
The shard-borne beetle with his drowsy hums
Hath rung night's yawning peal, there shall be done
A deed of dreadful note.

50 **Lady Macbeth.** What's to be done?

Macbeth. Be innocent of the knowledge, dearest chuck,
Till thou applaud the deed. Come, seeling night,
Scarf up the tender eye of pitiful day,
And with thy bloody and invisible hand
55 Cancel and tear to pieces that great bond
Which keeps me pale! Light thickens, and the crow
Makes wing to the rooky wood.
Good things of day begin to droop and drowse,
Whiles night's black agents to their preys do rouse.
60 Thou marvell'st at my words; but hold thee still:
Things bad begun make strong themselves by ill.
So prithee go with me.

[Exeunt.]

Scene 3 *A park near the palace.*

*The two murderers, joined by a third, ambush
Banquo and Fleance, killing Banquo. Fleance
manages to escape in the darkness.*

3-6 ***He needs . . . just:*** Macbeth should not be distrustful, since he gave us the orders (**offices**) and we plan to follow his directions exactly.

9 ***lated:*** tardy; late.

10 ***To gain . . . inn:*** to reach the inn before dark.

13 ***Give us a light:*** Banquo, nearing the palace, calls for servants to bring a light.

14-16 ***Then 'tis . . . court:*** It must be Banquo, since all the other expected guests are already in the palace.

17 ***His horses go about:*** Servants have taken his horses to the stable.

23 ***Stand to't:*** Be prepared.

27 ***Thou mayst revenge:*** You might live to avenge my death.

[Enter three Murderers.]

First Murderer. But who did bid thee join with us?

Third Murderer.   Macbeth.

Second Murderer. He needs not our mistrust, since he delivers
5   Our offices, and what we have to do,
     To the direction just.

First Murderer.   Then stand with us.
     The west yet glimmers with some streaks of day.
     Now spurs the lated traveler apace
10   To gain the timely inn, and near approaches
     The subject of our watch.

Third Murderer.   Hark! I hear horses.

Banquo. *[Within]* Give us a light there, ho!

Second Murderer.   Then 'tis he! The rest
15   That are within the note of expectation
     Already are i' the court.

First Murderer.   His horses go about.

Third Murderer. Almost a mile; but he does usually,
     So all men do, from hence to the palace gate
20   Make it their walk.

[Enter Banquo, and Fleance with a torch.]

Second Murderer.   A light, a light!

Third Murderer.   'Tis he.

First Murderer. Stand to't.

Banquo. It will be rain tonight.

25 **First Murderer.**   Let it come down!

[They set upon Banquo.]

Banquo. O, treachery! Fly, good Fleance, fly, fly, fly!
     Thou mayst revenge. O slave!

29 ***Was't not the way:*** Isn't that what we were supposed to do? Apparently, one of the murderers struck out the light, thus allowing Fleance to escape.

1 ***your own degrees:*** where your rank entitles you to sit.

[Dies. Fleance escapes.]

Third Murderer. Who did strike out the light?

First Murderer. Was't not the way?

30 **Third Murderer.** There's but one down; the son is fled.

Second Murderer. We have lost
Best half of our affair.

First Murderer. Well, let's away, and say how much is
done.

[Exeunt.]

Scene 4 *The hall in the palace.*

*As the banquet begins, one of the murderers
reports on Banquo's death and Fleance's
escape. Macbeth is disturbed by the news and
even more shaken when he returns to the
banquet table and sees the bloody ghost of
Banquo. Only Macbeth sees the ghost, and his
terrified reaction startles the guests. Lady
Macbeth explains her husband's strange
behavior as an illness from childhood that will
soon pass. Once the ghost disappears,
Macbeth calls for a toast to Banquo, whose
ghost immediately reappears. Because
Macbeth begins to rant and rave, Lady
Macbeth dismisses the guests, fearful that her
husband will reveal too much. Macbeth, alone
with his wife, tells of his suspicions of
Macduff, absent from the banquet. He also
says he will visit the witches again and hints at
bloody deeds yet to happen.*

[Banquet prepared. Enter Macbeth, Lady Macbeth, Ross,
Lennox, Lords, *and* Attendants.*]*

Macbeth. You know your own degrees, sit down. At first
And last the hearty welcome.

6 ***keeps her state:*** sits on her throne rather than at the banquet table.

11-16 ***measure:*** toast. Macbeth keeps talking to his wife and guests as he casually edges toward the door to speak privately with the murderer.

19 ***dispatched:*** killed.

24 ***nonpareil:*** best.

27 ***fit:*** fever of fear.

30 ***casing:*** surrounding.

Lords.   Thanks to your Majesty.

Macbeth. Ourself will mingle with society
5   And play the humble host.
       Our hostess keeps her state, but in best time
       We will require her welcome.

Lady Macbeth. Pronounce it for me, sir, to all our
          friends,
10   For my heart speaks they are welcome.

[Enter First Murderer to the door.]

Macbeth. See, they encounter thee with their hearts'
          thanks.
       Both sides are even: here I'll sit i' the midst.
       Be large in mirth; anon we'll drink a measure
15   The table round. *[Moves toward Murderer at door.]*
       There's blood upon thy face.

Murderer. 'Tis Banquo's then.

Macbeth. 'Tis better thee without than he within.
       Is he dispatched?

20 **Murderer.** My lord, his throat is cut. That I did for him.

Macbeth. Thou art the best o' the cutthroats! Yet he's
          good
       That did the like for Fleance. If thou didst it,
       Thou art the nonpareil.

25 **Murderer.**   Most royal sir,
       Fleance is scaped.

Macbeth. *[Aside]* Then comes my fit again. I had else
          been perfect;
       Whole as the marble, founded as the rock,
30   As broad and general as the casing air.
       But now I am cabined, cribbed, confined, bound in
       To saucy doubts and fears.—But Banquo's safe?

35 ***The least . . . nature:*** even the smallest wound being enough to cause death.

37 ***worm:*** little serpent, that is, Fleance.

39 ***No teeth for the present:*** too young to cause harm right now. Contrast this comment with his privately expressed fears.

40 ***hear ourselves:*** talk together.

41-46 Macbeth must not forget his duties as host. A feast will be no different from a meal that one pays for unless the host gives his guests courteous attention (***ceremony***), the best part of any meal.

47 ***Sweet remembrancer:*** a term of affection for his wife, who has reminded him of his duty.

51-54 The best people of Scotland would all be under Macbeth's roof if Banquo were present too. He hopes Banquo's absence is due to rudeness rather than to some accident (***mischance***).

58 Macbeth finally notices that Banquo's ghost is present and sitting in the King's chair. As you read about this encounter, consider how Macbeth's reaction affects his guests.

Murderer. Ay, my good lord. Safe in a ditch he bides,
With twenty trenched gashes on his head,
35   The least a death to nature.

Macbeth.   Thanks for that!
There the grown serpent lies; the worm that's fled
Hath nature that in time will venom breed,
No teeth for the present. Get thee gone. Tomorrow
40   We'll hear ourselves again.

[Exit Murderer.]

Lady Macbeth.   My royal lord,
You do not give the cheer. The feast is sold
That is not often vouched, while 'tis a-making,
'Tis given with welcome. To feed were best at home.
45   From thence, the sauce to meat is ceremony;
Meeting were bare without it.

[Enter the Ghost of Banquo, and sits in Macbeth's place.]

Macbeth.   Sweet remembrancer!
Now good digestion wait on appetite,
And health on both!

50 **Lennox.**   May't please your Highness sit.

Macbeth. Here had we now our country's honor, roofed,
Were the graced person of our Banquo present;
Who may I rather challenge for unkindness
Than pity for mischance!

55 **Ross.**   His absence, sir,
Lays blame upon his promise. Please't your Highness
To grace us with your royal company?

Macbeth. The table's full.

Lennox.   Here is a place reserved, sir.

60 **Macbeth.** Where?

Lennox. Here, my good lord. What is't that moves
your Highness?

66 **gory:** ghostly.

68-73 **Sit . . . not:** Macbeth, confused and frantic, has seemed to be talking to thin air. Nervously, Lady Macbeth tries to calm the guests by claiming her husband often has such fits. She says the attack will pass quickly (**upon a thought**) and that looking at him will only make him worse (**extend his passion**). *Why does Lady Macbeth make up a story to tell the guests?*

76-84 She dismisses his hallucination as utter nonsense (**proper stuff**). His outbursts (**flaws and starts**) are the product of imaginary fears (**impostors to true fear**) and are unmanly, the kind of behavior described in a woman's story. *Do you think her appeal to his manhood will work this time?*

87 **canst nod:** The ghost has been shaking his head in accusation.

88-90 If burial vaults (**charnel houses**) give back the dead, then we may as well throw our bodies to the birds (**kites**), whose stomachs (**maws**) will become our tombs (**monuments**).

Macbeth. Which of you have done this?

Lords.   What, my good lord?

65 **Macbeth.** Thou canst not say I did it. Never shake
   Thy gory locks at me.

Ross. Gentlemen, rise. His Highness is not well.

Lady Macbeth. Sit, worthy friends. My lord is often thus,
   And hath been from his youth. Pray you keep seat.
70 The fit is momentary; upon a thought
   He will again be well. If much you note him,
   You shall offend him and extend his passion.
   Feed, and regard him not.—Are you a man?

Macbeth. Ay, and a bold one, that dare look on that
75 Which might appal the devil.

Lady Macbeth.   O proper stuff!
   This is the very painting of your fear.
   This is the air-drawn dagger which you said
   Led you to Duncan. O, these flaws and starts
80 (Impostors to true fear) would well become
   A woman's story at a winter's fire,
   Authorized by her grandam. Shame itself!
   Why do you make such faces? When all's done,
   You look but on a stool.

85 **Macbeth.** Prithee see there! behold! look! lo! How say
   you?
   Why, what care I? If thou canst nod, speak too.
   If charnel houses and our graves must send
   Those that we bury back, our monuments
90 Shall be the maws of kites.

[Exit Ghost.*]*

Lady Macbeth.   What, quite unmanned in folly?

Macbeth. If I stand here, I saw him.

Lady Macbeth.   Fie, for shame!

94-98 Macbeth desperately tries to justify his murder of Banquo. Murder has been common from ancient times to the present, though laws (**humane statute**) have tried to rid civilized society (**gentle weal**) of violence.

98-100 In the old days, people at least stayed dead when you killed them.

107 **muse:** wonder.

108 **infirmity:** sickness.

113-114 **To all . . . to all:** Macbeth toasts everyone, including Banquo.

115 **Our . . . pledge:** We toast our duties and loyalty to you.

116-120 **Avaunt:** go away. Macbeth sees Banquo again. He tells Banquo that he is only a ghost, with unreal bones, cold blood, and no consciousness (**speculation**).

122 **thing of custom:** a normal event.

124-132 Macbeth would be willing to face Banquo in any other form, even his living self. **If trembling . . . girl:** If I still tremble, call me a girl's doll.

Macbeth. Blood hath been shed ere now, i' the olden

95   time,

Ere humane statue purged the gentle weal;

Ay, and since too, murders have been performed

Too terrible for the ear. The time has been

That, when the brains were out, the man would die,

100   And there an end! But now they rise again,

With twenty mortal murders on their crowns,

And push us from our stools. This is more strange

Than such a murder is.

Lady Macbeth.   My worthy lord,

105   Your noble friends do lack you.

Macbeth.   I do forget.

Do not muse at me, my most worthy friends.

I have a strange infirmity, which is nothing

To those that know me. Come, love and health to all!

110   Then I'll sit down. Give me some wine, fill full.

[Enter Ghost.]

I drink to the general joy o' the whole table,

And to our dear friend Banquo, whom we miss.

Would he were here! To all, and him, we thirst,

And all to all.

115   **Lords.**   Our duties, and the pledge.

Macbeth. Avaunt, and quit my sight! Let the earth hide

thee!

Thy bones are marrowless, thy blood is cold;

Thou hast no speculation in those eyes

120   Which thou dost glare with!

Lady Macbeth.   Think of this, good peers,

But as a thing of custom. 'Tis no other.

Only it spoils the pleasure of the time.

Macbeth. What man dare, I dare.

125   Approach thou like the rugged Russian bear,

The armed rhinoceros, or the Hyrcan tiger;

137 *admired:* astonishing.

138-144 Macbeth is bewildered by his wife's calm after such an event. Her reaction makes him seem a stranger to himself (*strange / Even to the disposition that I owe*): she seems to be the one with all the courage, since he is white (*blanched*) with fear.

145 Everyone can hear Macbeth, which makes Lady Macbeth afraid that her husband will reveal too much.

149 *Stand . . . going:* Don't worry about the proper formalities of leaving.

154-159 Macbeth fears that Banquo's murder (*It*) will be revenged by his own murder. Stones, trees, or talking birds (*maggot-pies and choughs and rooks*) may reveal the hidden knowledge (*Augures*) of his guilt.

Take any shape but that, and my firm nerves
Shall never tremble. Or be alive again
And dare me to the desert with thy sword.
130 If trembling I inhabit then, protest me
The baby of a girl. Hence, horrible shadow!
Unreal mock'ry, hence!

[Exit Ghost.]

                     Why, so! Being gone,
I am a man again. Pray you sit still.

135 **Lady Macbeth.** You have displaced the mirth, broke the
      good meeting
With most admired disorder.

Macbeth.   Can such things be,
And overcome us like a summer's cloud
140 Without our special wonder? You make me strange
Even to the disposition that I owe,
When now I think you can behold such sights
And keep the natural ruby of your cheeks
When mine is blanched with fear.

145 **Ross.**   What sights, my lord?

Lady Macbeth. I pray you speak not. He grows worse and
      worse;
Question enrages him. At once, good night.
Stand not upon the order of your going,
150 But go at once.

Lennox.   Good night, and better health
Attend his Majesty!

Lady Macbeth.   A kind good night to all!

[Exeunt Lords and Attendants.]

Macbeth. It will have blood, they say: blood will have
155   blood.
Stones have been known to move and trees to speak;
Augures and understood relations have

162-163 *How say'st . . . bidding:* What do you think of Macduff's refusal to come? *Why do you think Macbeth is suddenly so concerned about Macduff?*

166-167 *There's . . . feed:* Macbeth has paid (*feed*) household servants to spy on every noble, including Macduff.

168 *betimes:* early.

169 *bent:* determined.

170-175 *For mine . . . scanned:* Macbeth will do anything to protect himself. He has stepped so far into a river of blood that it would make no sense to turn back. He will act upon his unnatural (*strange*) thoughts without having examined (*scanned*) them.

176 *season:* preservative.

177-179 His vision of the ghost (*strange and self-abuse*) is only the result of a beginner's fear (*initiate fear*), to be cured with practice (*hard use*).

By maggot-pies and choughs and rooks brought forth
The secret'st man of blood. What is the night?

160 **Lady Macbeth.** Almost at odds with morning, which is
      which.

Macbeth. How say'st thou that Macduff denies his person
      At our great bidding?

Lady Macbeth.   Did you send to him, sir?

165 **Macbeth.** I hear it by the way; but I will send.
      There's not a one of them but in his house
      I keep a servant feed. I will tomorrow
      (And betimes I will) to the Weird Sisters.
      More shall they speak; for now I am bent to know
170   By the worst means the worst. For mine own good
      All causes shall give way. I am in blood
      Stepped in so far that, should I wade no more,
      Returning were as tedious as go o'er.
      Strange things I have in head, that will to hand,
175   Which must be acted ere they may be scanned.

Lady Macbeth. You lack the season of all natures, sleep.

Macbeth. Come, we'll to sleep. My strange and self-abuse
      Is the initiate fear that wants hard use.
      We are yet but young in deed.

[Exeunt.]

Scene 5 *A heath.*

*The goddess of witchcraft, Hecate, scolds the three
witches for dealing independently with Macbeth. She
outlines their next meeting with him, planning to
cause his downfall by making him overconfident.
(Experts believe this scene was not written by
Shakespeare but rather was added later.)*

[Thunder. Enter the three Witches, *meeting* Hecate.*]*

2 *beldams:* hags.

7 *close contriver:* secret inventor.

13 *Loves . . . you:* cares only about his own goals, not about you.

15 *Acheron:* a river in hell, according to Greek mythology. Hecate plans to hold their meeting in a hellish place.

20-21 *This . . . end:* Tonight I'm working for a disastrous (*dismal*) and fatal end for Macbeth.

24-29 Hecate will obtain a magical drop from the moon, treat it with secret art, and so create spirits (*artificial sprites*) that will lead Macbeth to his destruction (*confusion*).

30-33 She predicts that he will become overconfident, convinced of his own security.

34-35 Like the other witches, Hecate has a demon helper (*my little spirit*). At the end of her speech, she is raised by pulley to the "Heavens" of the stage.

First Witch. Why, how now, Hecate? You look angerly.

Hecate. Have I not reason, beldams as you are,
    Saucy and overbold? How did you dare
    To trade and traffic with Macbeth
5   In riddles and affairs of death;
    And I, the mistress of your charms,
    The close contriver of all harms,
    Was never called to bear my part
    Or show the glory of our art?
10   And, which is worse, all you have done
    Hath been but for a wayward son,
    Spiteful and wrathful, who, as others do,
    Loves for his own ends, not for you.
    But make amends now. Get you gone
15   And at the pit of Acheron
    Meet me i' the morning. Thither he
    Will come to know his destiny.
    Your vessels and your spells provide,
    Your charms and everything beside.
20   I am for the air. This night I'll spend
    Unto a dismal and a fatal end.
    Great business must be wrought ere noon.
    Upon the corner of the moon
    There hangs a vap'rous drop profound.
25   I'll catch it ere it come to ground;
    And that, distilled by magic sleights,
    Shall raise such artificial sprites
    As by the strength of their illusion
    Shall draw him on to his confusion.
30   He shall spurn fate, scorn death, and bear
    His hopes 'bove wisdom, grace, and fear;
    And you all know security
    Is mortals' chiefest enemy.

[Music and a song within. "Come away, come away," etc.]

    Hark! I am called. My little spirit, see,
35   Sits in a foggy cloud and stays for me.

1-3 ***My former . . . borne:*** Lennox and the other lord had shared suspicions of Macbeth. Recent events carry their suspicions farther.

5 ***Marry:*** a mild oath. Lennox ironically suggests that Macbeth's affections lead to murder.

7-8 ***Whom . . . Fleance fled:*** Lennox is being ironic when he says that fleeing the scene of the crime must make Fleance guilty of his father's death.

9-11 ***Who . . . father:*** He says that everyone can agree on the horror of Duncan's being murdered by his sons. But Lennox has been consistently ironic, claiming to believe in what is obviously false. His words indirectly blame Macbeth.

13 ***pious:*** holy.

16-17 ***For 'twould . . . deny't:*** Again, he is being ironic. If the servants had lived, Macbeth might have been discovered.

[Exit.]

First Witch. Come, let's make haste. She'll soon be back
again.

[Exeunt.]

Scene 6 *The palace at Forres.*

*Lennox and another Scottish lord review the events
surrounding the murders of Duncan and Banquo,
indirectly suggesting that Macbeth is both a murderer
and a tyrant. It is reported that Macduff has gone to
England, where Duncan's son Malcolm is staying with
King Edward and raising an army to regain the
Scottish throne. Macbeth, angered by Macduff's
refusal to see him, is also preparing for war.*

[Enter Lennox *and another* Lord.*]*

Lennox. My former speeches have but hit your thoughts,
Which can interpret farther. Only I say
Things have been strangely borne. The gracious
     Duncan

5   Was pitied of Macbeth. Marry, he was dead!
And the right valiant Banquo walked too late;
Whom, you may say (if't please you) Fleance killed,
For Fleance fled. Men must not walk too late.
Who cannot want the thought how monstrous

10 It was for Malcolm and for Donalbain
To kill their gracious father? Damned fact!
How it did grieve Macbeth! Did he not straight,
In pious rage, the two delinquents tear,
That were the slaves of drink and thralls of sleep?

15 Was not that nobly done? Ay, and wisely too!
For 'twould have angered any heart alive
To hear the men deny't. So that I say
He has borne all things well; and I do think
That, had he Duncan's sons under his key

20 (As, an't please heaven, he shall not), they should find

22 *from broad words:* because of his frank talk.

25 *bestows himself:* is staying.

27 *From . . . birth:* Macbeth keeps Malcolm from his birthright. As the eldest son of Duncan, Malcolm should be king.

29 *Edward:* Edward the Confessor, king of England from 1042 to 1066, a man known for his virtue and religion.

30-31 *That . . . respect:* Though Malcolm suffers from bad fortune (the loss of the throne), he is respectfully treated by Edward.

31-39 *Thither . . . for now:* Macduff wants the King to persuade the people of Northumberland (an English county near Scotland) and their earl, Siward, to join Malcolm's cause. With their help Malcolm may be able to restore order and peace in Scotland.

39-41 *And . . . war:* Macbeth is so angry (*exasperate*) at these reports from England that he prepares for war.

43-46 The messenger, fearing Macbeth's anger, was unhappy (*cloudy*) with Macduff's refusal to cooperate. Because Macduff burdens (*clogs*) him with bad news, he will not hurry back.

49-54 *Some . . . accursed:* Lennox wants news of Macduff's appeal for military aid to arrive in England before Macduff himself, so that blessings may swiftly return to Scotland.

What 'twere to kill a father. So should Fleance.
But peace! for from broad words, and 'cause he failed
His presence at the tyrant's feast, I hear
Macduff lives in disgrace. Sir, can you tell
25   Where he bestows himself?

Lord.   The son of Duncan,
From whom this tyrant holds the due of birth,
Lives in the English court, and is received
Of the most pious Edward with such grace
30   That the malevolence of fortune nothing
Takes from his high respect. Thither Macduff
Is gone to pray the holy King upon his aid
To wake Northumberland and warlike Siward;
That by the help of these (with Him above
35   To ratify the work) we may again
Give to our tables meat, sleep to our nights,
Free from our feasts and banquets bloody knives,
Do faithful homage and receive free honors—
All which we pine for now. And this report
40   Hath so exasperate the King that he
Prepares for some attempt of war.

Lennox.   Sent he to Macduff?

Lord. He did; and with an absolute "Sir, not I!"
The cloudy messenger turns me his back
45   And hums, as who should say, "You'll rue the time
That clogs me with this answer."

Lennox.   And that well might
Advise him to a caution t' hold what distance
His wisdom can provide. Some holy angel
50   Fly to the court of England and unfold
His message ere he come, that a swift blessing
May soon return to this our suffering country
Under a hand accursed!

Lord.   I'll send my prayers with him.

[Exeunt.]

1-3 Magical signals and the call of the third witch's attending demon (**Harpier**) tell the witches to begin.

4-34 The witches are stirring up a magical stew to bring trouble to humanity. Their recipe includes intestines (**entrails, chaudron**), a slice (**Fillet**) of snake, eye of salamander (**newt**), snake tongue (**Adder's fork**), a lizard (**blindworm**), a baby owl's (**howlet's**) wing, a shark's stomach and gullet (**maw and gulf**), the finger of a baby strangled by a prostitute (**drab**), and other gruesome ingredients. They stir their brew until thick and slimy (**slab**).

ACT FOUR

Scene 1 *A cave. In the middle, a boiling cauldron.*

The three witches prepare a potion in a boiling kettle. When Macbeth arrives, demanding to know his future, the witches raise three apparitions. The first, an armed head, tells him to beware of Macduff. Next, a bloody child assures Macbeth that he will never be harmed by anyone born of woman. The third apparition tells him that he will never be defeated until the trees of Birnam Wood move toward his castle at Dunsinane. Macbeth, now confident of his future, asks about Banquo's son. His confidence fades when the witches show him a line of kings who all resemble Banquo, suggesting that Banquo's sons will indeed be kings. Macbeth curses the witches as they disappear.

Lennox enters the cave and tells Macbeth that Macduff has gone to the English court. Hearing this, Macbeth swears to kill Macduff's family.

[Thunder. Enter the three Witches.*]*

First Witch. Thrice the brinded cat hath mewed.

Second Witch. Thrice, and once the hedge-pig whined.

Third Witch. Harpier cries; 'tis time, 'tis time.

First Witch. Round about the cauldron go;
5   In the poisoned entrails throw.
    Toad, that under cold stone
    Days and nights has thirty-one
    Swelt'red venom sleeping got,
    Boil thou first i' the charmed pot.

Most experts believe that the entrance of Hecate and three more witches was not written by Shakespeare. The characters were probably added later to expand the role of the witches who were favorites of the audience.

10 **All.** Double, double, toil and trouble;
    Fire burn, and cauldron bubble.

    Second Witch. Fillet of a fenny snake,
    In the cauldron boil and bake;
    Eye of newt, and toe of frog,
15   Wool of bat, and tongue of dog,
    Adder's fork, and blindworm's sting,
    Lizard's leg, and howlet's wing;
    For a charm of pow'rful trouble
    Like a hell-broth boil and bubble.

20 **All.** Double, double, toil and trouble;
    Fire burn, and cauldron bubble.

    Third Witch. Scale of dragon, tooth of wolf,
    Witch's mummy, maw and gulf
    Of the ravined salt-sea shark,
25   Root of hemlock, digged i' the dark;
    Liver of blaspheming Jew,
    Gall of goat, and slips of yew
    Slivered in the moon's eclipse;
    Nose of Turk and Tartar's lips;
30   Finger of birth-strangled babe
    Ditch-delivered by a drab:
    Make the gruel thick and slab.
    Add thereto a tiger's chaudron
    For the ingredience of our cauldron.

35 **All.** Double, double, toil and trouble;
    Fire burn, and cauldron bubble.

    Second Witch. Cool it with a baboon's blood,
    Then the charm is firm and good.

[Enter Hecate and the other three Witches.]

    Hecate. O, well done! I commend your pains,
40   And every one shall share i' the gains.
    And now about the cauldron sing
    Like elves and fairies in a ring,
    Enchanting all that you put in.

51-62 Macbeth calls upon (***conjure***) the witches in the name of their dark magic (***that which you profess***). Though they unleash winds to topple churches and make foaming (***yesty***) waves to destroy (***Confound***) ships, though they flatten wheat (***corn***) fields, destroy buildings, and reduce nature's order to chaos by mixing all seeds (***germens***) together, he demands an answer to his question. *How has Macbeth's attitude toward the witches changed from his earlier meetings?*

68 *masters:* the demons whom the witches serve.

71 *farrow:* newborn pigs; ***grease . . . gibbet:*** grease from a gallows where a murderer was hung.

[Music and a song, "Black spirit," etc.]

Second Witch. By the pricking of my thumbs,

45   Something wicked this way comes.
               Open locks,
               Whoever knocks!

[Enter Macbeth.]

Macbeth. How now, you secret, black, and midnight hags?
     What is't you do?

50 **All.**   A deed without a name.

Macbeth. I conjure you by that which you profess
     (Howe'er you come to know it), answer me.
     Though you untie the winds and let them fight
     Against the churches; though the yesty waves
55   Confound and swallow navigation up;
     Though bladed corn be lodged and trees blown down;
     Though castles topple on their warders' heads;
     Though palaces and pyramids do slope
     Their heads to their foundations; though the treasure
60   Of nature's germens tumble all together,
     Even till destruction sicken—answer me
     To what I ask you.

First Witch.   Speak.

Second Witch.   Demand.

65 **Third Witch.**   We'll answer.

First Witch. Say, if th' hadst rather hear it from our
     mouths
     Or from our masters.

Macbeth.   Call 'em! Let me see 'em.

70 **First Witch.** Pour in sow's blood, that hath eaten
     Her nine farrow; grease that's sweaten
     From the murderer's gibbet throw
     Into the flame.

75 *office:* function.

Each of the three apparitions holds a clue to Macbeth's future. *What do you think is suggested by the armed head?*

83 *harped:* guessed. The apparition has confirmed Macbeth's fears of Macduff.

Who or what might the bloody child represent?

89-92 *How do you think this prophecy will affect Macbeth?*

94-95 Despite the prophecy's apparent promise of safety, Macbeth decides to seek double insurance. The murder of Macduff will give Macbeth a guarantee (**bond**) of his fate and put his fears to rest.

Who or what might the child crowned represent?

All. Come, high or low;
75　Thyself and office deftly show!

[Thunder. First Apparition, an Armed Head.]

Macbeth. Tell me, thou unknown power—

First Witch. He knows thy thought.
Hear his speech, but say thou naught.

First Apparition. Macbeth! Macbeth! Macbeth! Beware
80　Macduff;
Beware the Thane of Fife. Dismiss me. Enough.

[He descends.]

Macbeth. Whate'er thou art, for thy good caution thanks!
Thou hast harped my fear aright. But one word
more—

85　**First Witch.** He will not be commanded. Here's another,
More potent than the first.

[Thunder. Second Apparition, a Bloody Child.]

Second Apparition. Macbeth! Macbeth! Macbeth!

Macbeth. Had I three ears, I'ld hear thee.

Second Apparition. Be bloody, bold, and resolute; laugh
90　to scorn
The pow'r of man, for none of woman born
Shall harm Macbeth.

[Descends.]

Macbeth. Then live, Macduff. What need I fear of thee?
But yet I'll make assurance double sure
95　And take a bond of fate. Thou shalt not live!
That I may tell pale-hearted fear it lies
And sleep in spite of thunder.

[Thunder. Third Apparition, a Child Crowned, with a tree in his hand.]

99 *issue:* children.

100-101 *the round / And top:* the crown.

103-108 The third apparition tells Macbeth to take courage. He cannot be defeated unless Birnam Wood travels the twelve-mile distance to Dunsinane Hill where his castle is located.

110 *impress:* force into service.

111 *bodements:* prophecies.

112-115 *Rebellious . . . custom:* Macbeth boasts that he will never again be troubled by ghosts (*Rebellious dead*) and that he will live out his expected lifespan (*lease of nature*). He believes he will die (*pay his breath*) by natural causes (*mortal custom*).

122 *Why . . . this:* The cauldron is sinking from sight to make room for the next apparition.
Macbeth next sees a procession (*show*) of eight kings, the last carrying a mirror (*glass*). According to legend, Fleance escaped to England, where he founded the Stuart family. James I of England, the king when this play was first performed, was the eighth Stuart king, the first to rule over both England and Scotland.

What is this
That rises like the issue of a king
100 And wears upon his baby-brow the round
And top of sovereignty?

All. Listen, but speak not to't.

Third Apparition. Be lion-mettled, proud, and take no
care
105 Who chafes, who frets, or where conspirers are.
Macbeth shall never vanquished be until
Great Birnam Wood to high Dunsinane Hill
Shall come against him. *[Descends.]*

Macbeth. That will never be.
110 Who can impress the forest, bid the tree
Unfix his earth-bound root? Sweet bodements, good!
Rebellious dead rise never till the Wood
Of Birnam rise, and our high-placed Macbeth
Shall live the lease of nature, pay his breath
115 To time and mortal custom. Yet my heart
Throbs to know one thing. Tell me, if your art
Can tell so much—shall Banquo's issue ever
Reign in this kingdom?

All. Seek to know no more.

120 **Macbeth.** I will be satisfied. Deny me this,
And an eternal curse fall on you! Let me know.
Why sinks that cauldron? and what noise is this?

[Hautboys.]

First Witch. Show!

Second Witch. Show!

125 **Third Witch.** Show!

All. Show his eyes, and grieve his heart!
Come like shadows, so depart!

*[A show of eight Kings, the eighth with a glass in his hand,
and* Banquo *last.]*

128-141 Macbeth is outraged that all eight kings in the procession look like Banquo. The mirror held by the last one shows a future with many more Banquo look-alikes as kings. The **twofold balls and treble scepters** pictured in the mirror foretell the union of Scotland and England in 1603, the year that James became king of both realms. Banquo, his hair matted (**boltered**) with blood, claims all the kings as his descendants. *What do you think is going through Macbeth's mind?*

142-149 Macbeth stands silent with amazement (**amazedly**). To cheer his spirits (**sprites**), the witches perform a weird circle dance (**antic round**).

150-152 *pernicious:* deadly, destructive. **aye:** always. After the witches vanish, Macbeth hears noises outside the cave and calls out.

Macbeth. Thou art too like the spirit of Banquo. Down!
Thy crown does sear mine eyeballs. And thy hair,
130 Thou other gold-bound brow, is like the first.
A third is like the former. Filthy hags!
Why do you show me this? A fourth? Start, eyes!
What, will the line stretch out to the crack of doom?
Another yet? A seventh? I'll see no more.
135 And yet the eighth appears, who bears a glass
Which shows me many more; and some I see
That twofold balls and treble scepters carry.
Horrible sight! Now I see 'tis true;
For the blood-boltered Banquo smiles upon me
140 And points at them for his. *[Apparitions descend.]* What?
Is this so?

First Witch. Ay, sir, all this is so. But why
Stands Macbeth thus amazedly?
Come, sisters, cheer we up his sprites
145 And show the best of our delights.
I'll charm the air to give a sound
While you perform your antic round,
That this great king may kindly say
Our duties did his welcome pay.

[Music. The Witches dance, and vanish.]

150 **Macbeth.** Where are they? Gone? Let this pernicious hour
Stand aye accursed in the calendar!
Come in, without there!

[Enter Lennox.]

Lennox. What's your Grace's will?

Macbeth. Saw you the Weird Sisters?

155 **Lennox.** No, my lord.

Macbeth. Came they not by you?

Lennox. No indeed, my lord.

Macbeth. Infected be the air whereon they ride,

165-179 Frustrated in his desire to kill Macduff, Macbeth blames his own hesitation, which gave his enemy time to flee. He concludes that one's plans (***flighty purpose***) are never achieved (***o'ertook***) unless carried out at once. From now on, Macbeth promises, he will act immediately on his impulses (***firstlings of my heart***) and complete (***crown***) his thoughts with acts. He will surprise Macduff's castle at Fife and kill his wife and children. *Why does Macbeth decide to kill Macduff's family?*

And damned all those that trust them! I did hear
160   The galloping of horse. Who was't came by?

Lennox. 'Tis two or three, my lord, that bring you word
    Macduff is fled to England.

Macbeth.   Fled to England?

Lennox. Ay, my good lord.

165 **Macbeth.** *[Aside]* Time, thou anticipat'st my dread
      exploits.
    The flighty purpose never is o'ertook
    Unless the deed go with it. From this moment
    The very firstlings of my heart shall be
170   The firstlings of my hand. And even now,
    To crown my thoughts with acts, be it thought and
      done!
    The castle of Macduff I will surprise,
    Seize upon Fife, give to the edge o' the sword
175   His wife, his babes, and all unfortunate souls
    That trace him in his line. No boasting like a fool!
    This deed I'll do before this purpose cool.
    But no more sights!—Where are these gentlemen?
    Come, bring me where they are.

Scene 2 *Macduff's castle at Fife.*

*Ross visits Lady Macduff to assure her of her
husband's wisdom and courage. Lady Macduff
cannot be comforted, believing that he left out
of fear. After Ross leaves she tells her son, who
is still loyal to his father, that Macduff was a
traitor and is now dead. A messenger warns
them to flee but is too late. Murderers sent by
Macbeth burst in, killing both wife and son.*

[Enter Lady Macduff, *her* Son, *and* Ross.*]*

Lady Macduff. What had he done to make him fly the
    land?

5-6 ***When our . . . traitors:*** Macduff's wife is worried that others will think her husband a traitor because his fears made him flee the country (***Our fears do make us traitors***), though he was guilty of no wrongdoing.

13 ***wants the natural touch:*** lacks the instinct to protect his family.

16-19 ***All . . . reason:*** Lady Macduff believes her husband is motivated entirely by fear, not by love of his family. His hasty flight is contrary to reason.

19-20 ***coz:*** cousin, a term used for any close relation; ***school:*** control; ***for:*** as for.

22 ***fits o' the season:*** disorders of the present time.

23-30 ***But . . . were before:*** Ross laments the cruelty of the times that made Macduff flee. In such times, people are treated like traitors for no reason. Their fears make them believe (***hold***) rumors, though they do not know what to fear and drift aimlessly like ships tossed by a tempest. Ross promises Lady Macduff he will return and assures her that the bad times will either end or improve (***climb upward***). He concludes by blessing Macduff's son.

33-35 Moved by pity for Macduff's family, Ross is near tears (***my disgrace***). He will leave before he embarrasses himself.

36-37 *Why does Lady Macduff tell her son that his father is dead, though the boy heard her discussion with Ross?*

Ross. You must have patience, madam.

Lady Macduff.   He had none.
5   His flight was madness. When our actions do not,
     Our fears do make us traitors.

Ross.   You know not
     Whether it was his wisdom or his fear.

Lady Macduff. Wisdom? To leave his wife, to leave his
10   babes,
     His mansion, and his titles, in a place
     From whence himself does fly? He loves us not,
     He wants the natural touch. For the poor wren,
     (The most diminutive of birds) will fight,
15   Her young ones in her nest, against the owl.
     All is the fear, and nothing is the love,
     As little is the wisdom, where the flight
     So runs against all reason.

Ross.   My dearest coz,
20   I pray you school yourself. But for your husband,
     He is noble, wise, judicious, and best knows
     The fits o' the season. I dare not speak much further;
     But cruel are the times, when we are traitors
     And do not know ourselves; when we hold rumor
25   From what we fear, yet know not what we fear,
     But float upon a wild and violent sea
     Each way and move—I take my leave of you.
     Shall not be long but I'll be here again.
     Things at the worst will cease, or else climb upward
30   To what they were before.—My pretty cousin,
     Blessing upon you!

Lady Macduff. Fathered he is, and yet he's fatherless.

Ross. I am so much a fool, should I stay longer,
     It would be my disgrace and your discomfort.
35   I take my leave at once.   *[Exit.]*

Lady Macduff.   Sirrah, your father's dead;
     And what will you do now? How will you live?

38-45 The spirited son refuses to be defeated by their bleak situation. He will live as birds do, taking whatever comes his way. His mother responds in kind, calling attention to devices used to catch birds: nets, sticky birdlime (*lime*), snares (*pitfall*), and traps (*gin*). The boy playfully answers that he has nothing to fear because no one sets a trap for a worthless bird.

50-54 Lady Macduff and her son affectionately joke about her ability to find a new husband. She expresses admiration for his intelligence (***With wit enough***).

55-65 Continuing his banter, the son asks if his father is a traitor. Lady Macduff, understandably hurt and confused by her husband's unexplained departure, answers yes.

Son. As birds do, mother.

Lady Macduff.　　　　　What, with worms and flies?

40　**Son.** With what I get, I mean; and so do they.

Lady Macduff. Poor bird! thou'dst never fear the net
　　nor lime,
　The pitfall nor the gin.

Son. Why should I, mother? Poor birds they are not set
45　　for.
　My father is not dead, for all your saying.

Lady Macduff. Yes, he is dead. How wilt thou do for a
　father?

Son. Nay, how will you do for a husband?

50　**Lady Macduff.** Why, I can buy me twenty at any market.

Son. Then you'll buy 'em to sell again.

Lady Macduff. Thou speak'st with all thy wit; and yet, i'
　faith,
　With wit enough for thee.

55　**Son.** Was my father a traitor, mother?

Lady Macduff. Ay, that he was!

Son. What is a traitor?

Lady Macduff. Why, one that swears, and lies.

Son. And be all traitors that do so?

60　**Lady Macduff.** Every one that does so is a traitor and
　　must be hanged.

Son. And must they all be hanged that swear and lie?

Lady Macduff. Every one.

Son. Who must hang them?

65　**Lady Macduff.** Why, the honest men.

66-74 Her son points out that traitors far outnumber honest men in this troubled time. The mother's terms of affection, **monkey** and **prattler** (childish talker), suggest that his playfulness has won her over.

75-83 The messenger, who knows Lady Macduff is an honorable person (**in your state of honor I am perfect**), delivers a polite but desperate warning, urging her to flee immediately. While he apologizes for scaring her, he warns that she faces a deadly (**fell**) cruelty, one dangerously close (**too nigh**).

87 *laudable:* praiseworthy.

92 *unsanctified:* unholy.

95 *shag-eared:* long-haired. Note how quickly the son reacts to the word traitor. *How do you think he feels about his father?*

Son. Then the liars and swearers are fools; for there are liars and swearers enow to beat the honest men and hang up them.

Lady Macduff. Now God help thee, poor monkey!
70 But how wilt thou do for a father?

Son. If he were dead, you'ld weep for him. If you would not, it were a good sign that I should quickly have a new father.

Lady Macduff. Poor prattler, how thou talk'st!

[Enter a Messenger.]

75 **Messenger.** Bless you, fair dame! I am not to you known,
Though in your state of honor I am perfect.
I doubt some danger does approach you nearly.
If you will take a homely man's advice,
Be not found here. Hence with your little ones!
80 To fright you thus methinks I am too savage;
To do worse to you were fell cruelty,
Which is too nigh your person. Heaven preserve you!
I dare abide no longer.   *[Exit.]*

Lady Macduff.   Whither should I fly?
85 I have done no harm. But I remember now
I am in this earthly world, where to do harm
Is often laudable, to do good sometime
Accounted dangerous folly. Why then, alas,
Do I put up that womanly defense
90 To say I have done no harm?—What are these faces?

[Enter Murderers.]

Murderer. Where is your husband?

Lady Macduff. I hope, in no place so unsanctified
Where such as thou mayst find him.

Murderer.   He's a traitor.

95 **Son.** Thou liest, thou shag-eared villain!

97 *Young fry:* small fish.

1-9 In response to Malcolm's depression about Scotland, Macduff advises that they grab a deadly (***mortal***) sword and defend their homeland (***birthdom***), as a soldier might stand over a fallen (***downfall'n***) comrade to protect him. The anguished cries of Macbeth's victims strike heaven and make the skies echo with cries of sorrow (***syllable of dolor***).

10-18 Malcolm's response shows his skeptical caution. He will grieve only for what he knows to be true; he will strike back only if the time is right (***As I shall find the time to friend***). Macduff may be honorable (***honest***), but he may be deceiving Malcolm to gain a reward from Macbeth (***something / You may discern of him through me***).

Murderer.   What, you egg!

[Stabbing him.]

   Young fry of treachery!

Son.   He has killed me, mother.
   Run away, I pray you!   *[Dies.]*

[Exit Lady Macduff, *crying "Murder!" followed by*
Murderers.*]*

Scene 3 England. *Before King Edward's palace.*

   Macduff urges Malcolm to join him in an invasion
   of Scotland, where the people suffer under
   Macbeth's harsh rule. Since Malcolm is uncertain
   of Macduff's motives, he tests him to see what
   kind of king Macduff would support. Once
   convinced of Macduff's honesty, Malcolm tells him
   that he has ten thousand soldiers ready to launch
   an attack. Ross arrives to tell them that some
   revolts against Macbeth have already begun.
   Reluctantly, Ross tells Macduff about the murder
   of his family. Wild with grief, Macduff vows to
   confront Macbeth and avenge the murders.

[Enter Malcolm *and* Macduff.*]*

Malcolm. Let us seek out some desolate shade, and there
   Weep our sad bosoms empty.

Macduff.   Let us rather
   Hold fast the mortal sword and, like good men,
5 Bestride our downfall'n birthdom. Each new morn
   New widows howl, new orphans cry, new sorrows
   Strike heaven on the face, that it resounds
   As if it felt with Scotland and yelled out
   Like syllable of dolor.

10 **Malcolm.**   What I believe, I'll wail;
   What know, believe; and what I can redress,
   As I shall find the time to friend, I will.

19-20 Macduff may betray the weak Malcolm, offering him
as a sacrifice to please an (***angry god***), Macbeth.

22-28 Malcolm further explains the reasons for his suspicions.
Even a good person may fall (***recoil***) into wickedness
because of a king's command (***imperial charge***). If
Macduff is innocent, he will not be harmed by these
suspicions, which cannot change (***transpose***) his
nature (***That which you are***). Virtue cannot be
damaged even by those who fall into evil, like Lucifer
(the ***brightest*** angel), and disguise themselves as
virtuous (***wear the brows of grace***). In contrast to
evil, virtue lives up to appearance.

30-37 Malcolm cannot understand how Macduff could leave
his family, a source of inspiration (***motives***) and love,
in an unprotected state (***rawness***). He asks him not to
be insulted by his suspicions (***jealousies***); Malcolm is
guarding his own safety.

38-45 Losing heart because of Malcolm's comments, Macduff
fears the worst for his country. Macbeth's tyranny can
lay a solid foundation (***basis***) because goodness, in the
person of Malcolm, will not stand against him.
Macbeth can enjoy ill-gotten gains now that his right
to the crown is confirmed (***affeered***). Macduff insists
that nothing could turn him into a villain.

47 ***I speak . . . of you:*** I am not certain that I need to
fear you.

What you have spoke, it may be so perchance.
This tyrant, whose sole name blisters our tongues,

15 Was once thought honest; you have loved him well;
He hath not touched you yet. I am young; but something
You may discern of him through me, and wisdom
To offer up a weak, poor, innocent lamb

20 T' appease an angry god.

Macduff. I am not treacherous.

Malcolm.   But Macbeth is.
A good and virtuous nature may recoil
In an imperial charge. But I shall crave your pardon.

25 That which you are, my thoughts cannot transpose.
Angels are bright still, though the brightest fell.
Though all things foul would wear the brows of grace,
Yet grace must still look so.

Macduff.   I have lost my hopes.

30 **Malcolm.** Perchance even there where I did find my doubts.
Why in that rawness left you wife and child,
Those precious motives, those strong knots of love,
Without leave-taking? I pray you,

35 Let not my jealousies be your dishonors,
But mine own safeties. You may be rightly just,
Whatever I shall think.

Macduff.   Bleed, bleed, poor country!
Great tyranny, lay thou thy basis sure,

40 For goodness dare not check thee! Wear thou thy wrongs;
The title is affeered! Fare thee well, lord.
I would not be the villain that thou think'st
For the whole space that's in the tyrant's grasp

45 And the rich East to boot.

Malcolm.   Be not offended.
I speak not as in absolute fear of you.

50-53 *I think . . . thousands:* Malcolm says that many people (**hands**) would join his cause and that the English have already offered thousands of men.

55-58 *yet my . . . succeed:* To test Macduff's honor and loyalty, Malcolm begins a lengthy description of his own fictitious vices. He suggests that Scotland may suffer more under his rule than under Macbeth's.

60-65 Malcolm says that his own vices are so plentiful and deeply planted (**grafted**) that Macbeth will seem innocent by comparison.

70 *Luxurious:* lustful.

71 *Sudden:* violent; *smacking:* tasting.

73 *voluptuousness:* lust.

75 *cistern:* large storage tank.

75-78 His lust is so great that it would overpower (**o'erbear**) all restraining obstacles (**continent impediments**).

79-89 Macduff offers an analysis of how Malcolm's lust may be controlled after he becomes king. Macduff describes uncontrolled desire (**Boundless intemperance**) as a tyrant of human nature that has caused the early (**untimely**) downfall of many kings. When Malcolm is king, however, he can still have his pleasures in abundance and fool everyone (**the time you may so hoodwink**) into believing that he is pure (**cold**). His lustful appetite (**vulture in you**) cannot be so great that it would not be satisfied by the many women willing to give themselves (**dedicate**) to a king. *Do you think Macduff's prediction is accurate?*

I think our country sinks beneath the yoke;
It weeps, it bleeds, and each new day a gash
50 Is added to her wounds. I think withal
There would be hands uplifted in my right;
And here from gracious England have I offer
Of goodly thousands. But, for all this,
When I shall tread upon the tyrant's head
55 Or wear it on my sword, yet my poor country
Shall have more vices than it had before,
More suffer and more sundry ways than ever,
By him that shall succeed.

Macduff.   What should he be?

60 **Malcolm.** It is myself I mean; in whom I know
All the particulars of vice so grafted
That, when they shall be opened, black Macbeth
Will seem as pure as snow, and the poor state
Esteem him as a lamb, being compared
65 With my confineless harms.

Macduff.   Not in the legions
Of horrid hell can come a devil more damned
In evils to top Macbeth.

Malcolm.   I grant him bloody,
70 Luxurious, avaricious, false, deceitful,
Sudden, malicious, smacking of every sin
That has a name. But there's no bottom, none,
In my voluptuousness. Your wives, your daughters,
Your matrons, and your maids could not fill up
75 The cistern of my lust; and my desire
All continent impediments would o'erbear
That did oppose my will. Better Macbeth
Than such an one to reign.

Macduff.   Boundless intemperance
80 In nature is a tyranny. It hath been
The untimely emptying of the happy throne
And fall of many kings. But fear not yet
To take upon you what is yours. You may

90-98 Malcolm adds insatiable greed (***stanchless avarice***) to the list of evils in his disposition (***affection***). If king, he would steal from his nobles, and his acquisitions (***more-having***) would only spur his desire for more. He would even invent excuses for destroying good nobles in order to seize their wealth.

99-105 Macduff recognizes that greed is a deeper-rooted problem than lust, which passes as quickly as the summer (***summer-seeming***). Many kings have been killed for their greed. But the King's property alone (***Of your mere own***) offers plenty (***foisons***) to satisfy his desire. Malcolm's vices can be tolerated (***are portable***) when balanced against his virtues. *Do you think Macduff's position is sensible?*

106-115 Malcolm claims that he lacks all the virtues appropriate to a king (***king-becoming graces***). His list of missing virtues includes truthfulness (***verity***), consistency (***stableness***), generosity (***Bounty***), humility (***lowliness***), and religious devotion. In contrast, his crimes are abundant and varied. He would shatter the world's peace and destroy all harmony (***concord***) if he could.

119-131 Macduff despairs at news of the apparent depth of Malcolm's evil. He can see no prospect of relief for Scotland's suffering under a tyrant who has no right to the throne (***untitled***). The rightful heir (***truest issue***), Malcolm, bans himself from the throne (***By his own interdiction***) because of his evil. Malcolm's vices slander his parents (***blaspheme his breed***)—his saintly father and his mother who renounced the world (***Died every day***) for the sake of her religion. Since Macduff will not help an evil man to become king, he will not be able to return to Scotland.

Convey your pleasures in a spacious plenty,
85 And yet seem cold—the time you may so hoodwink.
We have willing dames enough. There cannot be
That vulture in you to devour so many
As will to greatness dedicate themselves,
Finding it so inclined.

90 **Malcolm.**   With this there grows
In my most ill-composed affection such
A stanchless avarice that, were I King,
I should cut off the nobles for their lands,
Desire his jewels, and this other's house,
95 And my more-having would be as a sauce
To make me hunger more, that I should forge
Quarrels unjust against the good and loyal,
Destroying them for wealth.

Macduff.   This avarice
100 Sticks deeper, grows with more pernicious root
Than summer-seeming lust; and it hath been
The sword of our slain kings. Yet do not fear.
Scotland hath foisons to fill up your will
Of your mere own. All these are portable,
105 With other graces weighed.

Malcolm. But I have none. The king-becoming graces,
As justice, verity, temp'rance, stableness,
Bounty, perseverance, mercy, lowliness,
Devotion, patience, courage, fortitude,
110 I have no relish of them, but abound
In the division of each several crime,
Acting it many ways. Nay, had I pow'r, I should
Pour the sweet milk of concord into hell,
Uproar the universal peace, confound
115 All unity on earth.

Macduff.   O Scotland, Scotland!

Malcolm. If such a one be fit to govern, speak.
I am as I have spoken.

Macduff.   Fit to govern?

132-143 Macduff has finally convinced Malcolm of his honesty, removing all suspicions (***scruples***). Malcolm explains that his caution (***modest wisdom***) resulted from his fear of Macbeth's tricks. He takes back his accusations against himself (***Unspeak mine own detraction***) and renounces (***abjure***) the evils he previously claimed.

144-155 In fact, he is pure, sincere, and honest—a true servant of his country. He already has an army, ten thousand troops belonging to old Siward, the Earl of Northumberland. Now that Macduff is an ally, he hopes the battle's result will match the justice of their cause (***warranted quarrel***). *Why is Macduff left speechless by Malcolm's revelation?*

120   No, not to live. O nation miserable,
    With an untitled tyrant bloody-scept'red,
    When shalt thou see thy wholesome days again,
    Since that the truest issue of thy throne
    By his own interdiction stands accursed
125   And does blaspheme his breed? Thy royal father
    Was a most sainted king; the queen that bore thee,
    Oft'ner upon her knees than on her feet,
    Died every day she lived. Fare thee well!
    These evils thou repeat'st upon thyself
130   Have banished me from Scotland. O my breast,
    Thy hope ends here!

Malcolm.   Macduff, this noble passion,
    Child of integrity, hath from my soul
    Wiped the black scruples, reconciled my thoughts
135   To thy good truth and honor. Devilish Macbeth
    By many of these trains hath sought to win me
    Into his power; and modest wisdom plucks me
    From over-credulous haste; but God above
    Deal between thee and me! for even now
140   I put myself to thy direction and
    Unspeak mine own detraction, here abjure
    The taints and blames I laid upon myself
    For strangers to my nature. I am yet
    Unknown to woman, never was forsworn,
145   Scarcely have coveted what was mine own,
    At no time broke my faith, would not betray
    The devil to his fellow, and delight
    No less in truth than life. My first false speaking
    Was this upon myself. What I am truly,
150   Is thine and my poor country's to command;
    Whither indeed, before thy here-approach,
    Old Siward with ten thousand warlike men
    Already at a point was setting forth.
    Now we'll together; and the chance of goodness
155   Be like our warranted quarrel! Why are you silent?

Macduff. Such welcome and unwelcome things at once
    'Tis hard to reconcile.

160-180 Edward the Confessor, King of England, could reportedly heal the disease of scrofula (***the evil***) by his saintly touch. The doctor describes people who cannot be helped by medicine's best efforts (***The great assay of art***) waiting for the touch of the King's hand. Edward has cured many victims of this disease. Each time, he hangs a gold coin around their necks and offers prayers, a healing ritual that he will teach to his royal descendants (***succeeding royalty***).

184-185 ***Good God . . . strangers:*** May God remove Macbeth, who is the cause (***means***) of our being strangers.

[Enter a Doctor.]

Malcolm. Well, more anon. Comes the King forth, I pray
   you?

160 **Doctor.** Ay, sir. There are a crew of wretched souls
   That stay his cure. Their malady convinces
   The great assay of art; but at his touch,
   Such sanctity hath heaven given his hand,
   They presently amend.

165 **Malcolm.**   I thank you, doctor.

[Exit Doctor.]

Macduff. What's the disease he means?

Malcolm.   'Tis called the evil:
   A most miraculous work in this good king,
   Which often since my here-remain in England
170 I have seen him do. How he solicits heaven
   Himself best knows; but strangely-visited people,
   All swol'n and ulcerous, pitiful to the eye,
   The mere despair of surgery, he cures,
   Hanging a golden stamp about their necks,
175 Put on with holy prayers; and 'tis spoken,
   To the succeeding royalty he leaves
   The healing benediction. With this strange virtue,
   He hath a heavenly gift of prophecy,
   And sundry blessings hang about his throne
180 That speak him full of grace.

[Enter Ross.]

Macduff.   See who comes here.

Malcolm. My countryman; but yet I know him not.

Macduff. My ever gentle cousin, welcome hither.

Malcolm. I know him now. Good God betimes remove
185 The means that makes us strangers!

188-197 Ross describes Scotland's terrible condition. In a land where screams have become so common that they go unnoticed (***Are made, not marked***), violent sorrow becomes a commonplace emotion (***modern ecstasy***). So many have died that people no longer ask for their names, and good men die before their time.

198-199 ***relation / Too nice:*** news that is too accurate.

201-202 If the news is more than an hour old, listeners hiss at the speaker for being outdated; every minute gives birth to a new grief.

208 ***well at peace:*** Ross knows about the murder of Macduff's wife and son, but the news is too terrible to report.

211-217 Notice how Ross avoids the subject of Macduff's family. He mentions the rumors of nobles who are rebelling (***out***) against Macbeth. Ross believes the rumors because he saw Macbeth's troops on the march (***tyrant's power afoot***). The presence (***eye***) of Malcolm and Macduff in Scotland would help raise soldiers and remove (***doff***) Macbeth's evil (***dire distresses***).

Ross. Sir, amen.

Macduff. Stands Scotland where it did?

Ross. Alas, poor country,
Almost afraid to know itself! It cannot
190 Be called our mother, but our grave; where nothing,
But who knows nothing, is once seen to smile;
Where sighs and groans, and shrieks that rent the air,
Are made, not marked; where violent sorrow seems
A modern ecstasy. The dead man's knell
195 Is there scarce asked for who; and good men's lives
Expire before the flowers in their caps,
Dying or ere they sicken.

Macduff. O, relation
Too nice, and yet too true!

200 **Malcolm.** What's the newest grief?

Ross. That of an hour's age doth hiss the speaker;
Each minute teems a new one.

Macduff. How does my wife?

Ross. Why, well.

205 **Macduff.** And all my children?

Ross. Well too.

Macduff. The tyrant has not battered at their peace?

Ross. No, they were well at peace when I did leave 'em.

Macduff. Be not a niggard of your speech. How goes't?

210 **Ross.** When I came hither to transport the tidings
Which I have heavily borne, there ran a rumor
Of many worthy fellows that were out;
Which was to my belief witnessed the rather
For that I saw the tyrant's power afoot.
215 Now is the time of help. Your eye in Scotland
Would create soldiers, make our women fight
To doff their dire distresses.

221-222 ***An older . . . gives out:*** There is no soldier with a better reputation or more experience than Siward.

225 ***would:*** should.

226 ***latch:*** catch.

228 ***fee-grief:*** private sorrow.

230-231 ***No mind . . . woe:*** Every honorable (***honest***) person shares in this sorrow.

240-242 ***To relate . . . of you:*** Ross won't add to Macduff's sorrow by telling him how his family was killed. He compares Macduff's dear ones to the piled bodies of killed deer (***quarry***).

245-246 ***The grief . . . break:*** Silence will only push an overburdened heart to the breaking point.

250 Macduff laments his absence from the castle.

Malcolm.   Be't their comfort
We are coming thither. Gracious England hath
220   Lent us good Siward and ten thousand men.
An older and a better soldier none
That Christendom gives out.

Ross.   Would I could answer
This comfort with the like! But I have words
225   That would be howled out in the desert air,
Where hearing should not latch them.

Macduff.   What concern they?
The general cause? or is it a fee-grief
Due to some single breast?

230   **Ross.**   No mind that's honest
But in it shares some woe, though the main part
Pertains to you alone.

Macduff.   If it be mine,
Keep it not from me, quickly let me have it.

235   **Ross.** Let not your ears despise my tongue for ever,
Which shall possess them with the heaviest sound
That ever yet they heard.

Macduff.   Humh! I guess at it.

Ross. Your castle is surprised; your wife and babes
240   Savagely slaughtered. To relate the manner
Were, on the quarry of these murdered deer,
To add the death of you.

Malcolm.   Merciful heaven!
What, man! Ne'er pull your hat upon your brows.
245   Give sorrow words. The grief that does not speak
Whispers the o'erfraught heart and bids it break.

Macduff. My children too?

Ross.   Wife, children, servants, all
That could be found.

250   **Macduff.**   And I must be from thence?

256-259 *He has no children:* possibly a reference to Macbeth, who has no children to be killed for revenge. Macduff compares Macbeth to a bird of prey (*hell-kite*) who kills defenseless chickens and their mother.

266 *Naught:* nothing.

269 *whetstone:* grindstone used for sharpening.

271-276 *I could play . . . him too:* Macduff won't act like a woman by crying or like a braggart by boasting. He wants no delay (*intermission*) to keep him from face-to-face combat with Macbeth. Macduff ironically swears that, if Macbeth escapes, he deserves heaven's mercy.

277-282 Our troops are ready to attack, needing only the King's permission (*Our lack is nothing but our leave*). Like a ripe fruit, Macbeth is ready to fall, and heavenly powers are preparing to assist us. The long night of Macbeth's evil will be broken.

My wife killed too?

Ross. I have said.

Malcolm. Be comforted.
Let's make us med'cines of our great revenge
255 To cure this deadly grief.

Macduff. He has no children. All my pretty ones?
Did you say all? O hell-kite! All?
What, all my pretty chickens and their dam
At one fell swoop?

260 **Malcolm.** Dispute it like a man.

Macduff. I shall do so;
But I must also feel it as a man.
I cannot but remember such things were
That were most precious to me. Did heaven look on
265 And would not take their part? Sinful Macduff,
They were all struck for thee! Naught that I am,
Not for their own demerits, but for mine,
Fell slaughter on their souls. Heaven rest them now!

Malcolm. Be this the whetstone of your sword. Let grief
270 Convert to anger; blunt not the heart, enrage it.

Macduff. O, I could play the woman with mine eyes
And braggart with my tongue! But, gentle heavens,
Cut short all intermission. Front to front
Bring thou this fiend of Scotland and myself.
275 Within my sword's length set him. If he scape,
Heaven forgive him too!

Malcolm. This tune goes manly.
Come, go we to the King. Our power is ready;
Our lack is nothing but our leave. Macbeth
280 Is ripe for shaking, and the pow'rs above
Put on their instruments. Receive what cheer you may.
The night is long that never finds the day.

[Exeunt.]

4 ***went into the field:*** went to battle.

9-10 ***A great . . . of watching:*** To behave as though awake (***watching***) while sleeping is a sign of a greatly troubled nature.

15 ***meet:*** appropriate.

16-17 The attendant won't repeat what Lady Macbeth has said because there are no other witnesses to confirm her report. *What is she worried about?*

ACT FIVE

Scene 1 *Macbeth's castle at Dunsinane.*

A sleepwalking Lady Macbeth is observed by a concerned attendant, or gentlewoman, and a doctor. Lady Macbeth appears to be washing imagined blood from her hands. Her actions and confused speech greatly concern the doctor, and he warns the attendant to keep an eye on Lady Macbeth, fearing that she will harm herself.

[Enter a Doctor of Physic *and a* Waiting Gentlewoman.*]*

Doctor. I have two nights watched with you, but can perceive no truth in your report. When was it she last walked?

Gentlewoman. Since his Majesty went into the field I have
5   seen her rise from her bed, throw her nightgown upon her, unlock her closet, take forth paper, fold it, write upon't, read it, afterwards seal it, and again return to bed; yet all this while in a most fast sleep.

Doctor. A great perturbation in nature, to receive at once
10   the benefit of sleep and do the effects of watching! In this slumb'ry agitation, besides her walking and other actual performances, what (at any time) have you heard her say?

Gentlewoman. That, sir, which I will not report after her.

15 **Doctor.** You may to me, and 'tis most meet you should.

Gentlewoman. Neither to you nor any one, having no witness to confirm my speech.

[Enter Lady Macbeth, *with a taper.]*

18-19 *guise:* usual manner; ***stand close:*** hide yourself.

20 ***that light:*** her candle.

21-22 *Why might Lady Macbeth want a light by her at all times?*

34-39 Lady Macbeth's mind wanders as she repeats the motions of washing her hands. She refers to hell's darkness, then she relives how she persuaded her husband to murder Duncan; she had believed that their power would keep them from being held accountable (***accompt***). Finally, she envisions herself covered with Duncan's blood.

41-44 Lady Macbeth shows guilt about Macduff's wife. Then she addresses her husband, as if he were having another ghostly fit (***starting***).

Lo you, here she comes! This is her very guise, and, upon my life, fast asleep! Observe her; stand close.

20 **Doctor.** How came she by that light?

Gentlewoman. Why, it stood by her. She has light by her continually. 'Tis her command.

Doctor. You see her eyes are open.

Gentlewoman. Ay, but their sense is shut.

25 **Doctor.** What is it she does now? Look how she rubs her hands.

Gentlewoman. It is an accustomed action with her, to seem thus washing her hands. I have known her continue in this a quarter of an hour.

30 **Lady Macbeth.** Yet here's a spot.

Doctor. Hark, she speaks! I will set down what comes from her, to satisfy my remembrance the more strongly.

Lady Macbeth. Out, damned spot! out, I say! One; two. 35 Why then 'tis time to do't. Hell is murky. Fie, my lord, fie! a soldier, and afeard? What need we fear who knows it, when none can call our pow'r to accompt? Yet who would have thought the old man to have had so much blood in him?

40 **Doctor.** Do you mark that?

Lady Macbeth. The Thane of Fife had a wife. Where is she now? What, will these hands ne'er be clean? No more o' that, my lord, no more o' that! You mar all with this starting.

45 **Doctor.** Go to, go to! You have known what you should not.

Gentlewoman. She has spoke what she should not, I am sure of that. Heaven knows what she has known.

52 *sorely charged:* heavily burdened.

53-54 The gentlewoman says that she would not want Lady Macbeth's heavy heart in exchange for being queen.

57 *practice:* skill.

62 *on's:* of his.

63 *What has the doctor learned so far from Lady Macbeth's ramblings?*

69 *Foul whisp'rings are abroad:* Rumors of evil deeds are circulating.

72 She needs a priest more than a doctor.

74 *annoyance:* injury. The doctor may be worried about the possibility of Lady Macbeth's committing suicide.

76 *mated:* astonished.

Lady Macbeth. Here's the smell of the blood still. All the
perfumes of Arabia will not sweeten this little hand.
Oh, oh, oh!

Doctor. What a sigh is there! The heart is sorely charged.

Gentlewoman. I would not have such a heart in my
bosom for the dignity of the whole body.

Doctor. Well, well, well.

Gentlewoman. Pray God it be, sir.

Doctor. This disease is beyond my practice. Yet I have
known those which have walked in their sleep who
have died holily in their beds.

Lady Macbeth. Wash your hands, put on your nightgown,
look not so pale! I tell you yet again, Banquo's buried.
He cannot come out on's grave.

Doctor. Even so?

Lady Macbeth. To bed, to bed! There's knocking at the
gate. Come, come, come, come, give me your hand!
What's done cannot be undone. To bed, to bed, to bed!

[Exit.]

Doctor. Will she go now to bed?

Gentlewoman. Directly.

Doctor. Foul whisp'rings are abroad. Unnatural deeds
Do breed unnatural troubles. Infected minds
To their deaf pillows will discharge their secrets.
More needs she the divine than the physician.
God, God forgive us all! Look after her;
Remove from her the means of all annoyance,
And still keep eyes upon her. So good night.
My mind she has mated, and amazed my sight.
I think, but dare not speak.

Gentlewoman.   Good night, good doctor.

[Exeunt.]

3-5 ***for their dear . . . man:*** The cause of Malcolm and Macduff is so deeply felt that a dead (***mortified***) man would respond to their call to arms (***alarm***).

11-12 ***many . . . manhood:*** many soldiers who are too young to grow beards (***unrough***), that is, who have hardly reached manhood.

17-18 Like a man so swollen with disease (***distempered***) that he cannot buckle his belt, Macbeth cannot keep his evil actions under control.

21 Every minute, the revolts against Macbeth shame him for his treachery (***faith-breach***).

Scene 2 *The country near Dunsinane.*

The Scottish rebels, led by Menteith, Caithness, Angus, and Lennox, have come to Birnam Wood to join Malcolm and his English army. They know that Dunsinane has been fortified by a furious and brave Macbeth. They also know that his men neither love nor respect him.

[Drum and Colors. Enter Menteith, Caithness, Angus, Lennox, Soldiers.*]*

Menteith. The English pow'r is near, led on by Malcolm,
His uncle Siward, and the good Macduff.
Revenges burn in them; for their dear causes
Would to the bleeding and the grim alarm
5   Excite the mortified man.

Angus.   Near Birnam Wood
Shall we well meet them; that way are they coming.

Caithness. Who knows if Donalbain be with his brother?

Lennox. For certain, sir, he is not. I have a file
10   Of all the gentry. There is Siward's son
And many unrough youths that even now
Protest their first of manhood.

Menteith.   What does the tyrant?

Caithness. Great Dunsinane he strongly fortifies.
15   Some say he's mad; others, that lesser hate him,
Do call it valiant fury; but for certain
He cannot buckle his distempered cause
Within the belt of rule.

Angus.   Now does he feel
20   His secret murders sticking on his hands.
Now minutely revolts upbraid his faith-breach.
Those he commands move only in command,
Nothing in love. Now does he feel his title
Hang loose about him, like a giant's robe
25   Upon a dwarfish thief.

26-29 Macbeth's troubled nerves (***pestered senses***)—the product of his guilty conscience—have made him jumpy.

30-34 Caithness and the others will give their loyalty to the only help (***med' cine***) for the sick country (***weal***). They are willing to sacrifice their last drop of blood to cleanse (***purge***) Scotland.

35-37 Lennox compares Malcolm to a flower that needs the blood of patriots to water (***dew***) it and drown out weeds like Macbeth.

1-5 Macbeth wants no more news of thanes who have gone to Malcom's side.

6-11 Macbeth will not be infected (***taint***) with fear, because the witches (***spirits***), who know all human events (***mortal consequences***), have convinced him that he is invincible. He mocks the self-indulgent English (***English epicures***), then swears that he will never lack confidence.

Menteith. Who then shall blame
His pestered senses to recoil and start,
When all that is within him does condemn
Itself for being there?

30 **Caithness.** Well, march we on
To give obedience where 'tis truly owed.
Meet we the med'cine of the sickly weal;
And with him pour we in our country's purge
Each drop of us.

35 **Lennox.** Or so much as it needs
To dew the sovereign flower and drown the weeds.
Make we our march towards Birnam.

[Exeunt, marching.]

Scene 3 *Dunsinane. A room in the castle.*

*Macbeth awaits battle, confident of victory
because of what he learned from the witches.
After hearing that a huge army is ready to
march upon his castle, he expresses bitter
regrets about his life. While Macbeth prepares
for battle, the doctor reports that he cannot
cure Lady Macbeth, whose illness is mental,
not physical.*

[Enter Macbeth, Doctor, and Attendants.]

Macbeth. Bring me no more reports. Let them fly all!
Till Birnam Wood remove to Dunsinane,
I cannot taint with fear. What's the boy Malcolm?
Was he not born of woman? The spirits that know
5 All mortal consequences have pronounced me thus:
"Fear not, Macbeth. No man that's born of woman
Shall e'er have power upon thee." Then fly, false
    thanes,
And mingle with the English epicures.
10 The mind I sway by and the heart I bear

12-13 *loon:* stupid rascal; *goose look:* a look of fear.

17-20 Macbeth suggests that the servant cut his face so that blood will hide his cowardice. He repeatedly insults the servant, calling him a coward (*lily-livered*) and a clown (*patch*), and making fun of his white complexion (*linen cheeks, whey-face*).

24-32 *This push . . . dare not:* The upcoming battle will either make Macbeth secure (*cheer me ever*) or dethrone (*disseat*) him. He bitterly compares his life to a withered (*sere*) leaf. He cannot look forward to old age with its friends and honor, but only to curses and empty flattery (*mouth-honor, breath*) from those too timid (*the poor heart*) to tell the truth.

Shall never sag with doubt nor shake with fear.

[Enter Servant.]

The devil damn thee black, thou cream-faced loon!
Where got'st thou that goose look?

Servant. There is ten thousand—

15 **Macbeth.**   Geese, villain?

Servant.   Soldiers, sir.

Macbeth. Go prick thy face and over-red thy fear,
Thou lily-livered boy. What soldiers, patch?
Death of thy soul! Those linen cheeks of thine
20 Are counselors to fear. What soldiers, whey-face?

Servant. The English force, so please you.

Macbeth. Take thy face hence.

[Exit Servant.]

Seyton!—I am sick at heart,
When I behold—Seyton, I say!—This push
25 Will cheer me ever, or disseat me now.
I have lived long enough. My way of life
Is fallen into the sere, the yellow leaf;
And that which should accompany old age,
As honor, love, obedience, troops of friends,
30 I must not look to have; but, in their stead,
Curses not loud but deep, mouth-honor, breath,
Which the poor heart would fain deny, and dare not.
    Seyton!

[Enter Seyton.]

Seyton. What's your gracious pleasure?

35 **Macbeth.**   What news more?

Seyton. All is confirmed, my lord, which was reported.

Macbeth. I'll fight, till from my bones my flesh be hacked.
Give me my armor.

41 *mo:* more; *skirr:* scour.

47-53 Macbeth asks the doctor to remove the sorrow from Lady Macbeth's memory, to erase (*Raze out*) the troubles imprinted on her mind, and to relieve her overburdened heart (*stuffed bosom*) of its guilt (*perilous stuff*). *Do you think Macbeth shares his wife's feelings of guilt?*

56-66 Macbeth has lost his faith in the ability of medicine (*physic*) to help his wife. As he struggles into his armor, he says that if the doctor could successfully search the kingdom (*cast . . . land*) to find a cure for Lady Macbeth's disease, Macbeth would never stop praising him. *What kind of mood is Macbeth in?*

69-71 Macbeth leaves for battle, telling Seyton to bring the armour. He declares his fearlessness before death and destruction (*bane*).

Seyton.   'Tis not needed yet.

40 **Macbeth.** I'll put it on.
    Send out mo horses, skirr the country round;
    Hang those that talk of fear. Give me mine armor.
    How does your patient, doctor?

Doctor.   Not so sick, my lord,
45   As she is troubled with thick-coming fancies
    That keep her from her rest.

Macbeth.   Cure her of that!
    Canst thou not minister to a mind diseased,
    Pluck from the memory a rooted sorrow,
50   Raze out the written troubles of the brain,
    And with some sweet oblivious antidote
    Cleanse the stuffed bosom of that perilous stuff
    Which weighs upon the heart?

Doctor.   Therein the patient
55   Must minister to himself.

Macbeth. Throw physic to the dogs, I'll none of it!—
    Come, put mine armor on. Give me my staff.
    Seyton, send out.—Doctor, the thanes fly from me.—
    Come, sir, dispatch.—If thou couldst, doctor, cast
60   The water of my land, find her disease,
    And purge it to a sound and pristine health,
    I would applaud thee to the very echo,
    That should applaud again.—Pull't off, I say.—
    What rhubarb, senna, or what purgative drug,
65   Would scour these English hence? Hear'st thou of
      them?

Doctor. Ay, my good lord. Your royal preparation
    Makes us hear something.

Macbeth.   Bring it after me!
70   I will not be afraid of death and bane
    Till Birnam Forest come to Dunsinane.

6-9 Malcolm orders his men to cut down tree branches to camouflage themselves. This will conceal (**shadow**) the size of their army and confuse Macbeth's scouts. Consider the prophecy about Birnam Wood. *What do you now think the prophecy means?*

13 *setting down:* siege.

14-18 Malcolm says that men of all ranks (**Both more and less**) have abandoned Macbeth. Only weak men who have been forced into service remain with him.

Doctor. *[Aside]* Were I from Dunsinane away and clear,
Profit again should hardly draw me here.

[Exeunt.]

Scene 4 *The country near Birnam Wood.*

*The rebels and English forces have met in
Birnam Wood. Malcolm orders each soldier to
cut tree branches to camouflage himself. In
this way Birnam Wood will march upon
Dunsinane.*

[Drum and Colors. Enter Malcolm, Siward, Macduff,
Siward's Son, Menteith, Caithness, Angus, Lennox, Ross,
and Soldiers, *marching.]*

Malcolm. Cousins, I hope the days are near at hand
That chambers will be safe.

Menteith.   We doubt it nothing.

Siward. What wood is this before us?

5 **Menteith.**   The wood of Birnam.

Malcolm. Let every soldier hew him down a bough
And bear't before him. Thereby shall we shadow
The numbers of our host and make discovery
Err in report of us.

10 **Soldiers.**   It shall be done.

Siward. We learn no other but the confident tyrant
Keeps still in Dunsinane and will endure
Our setting down before't.

Malcolm.   'Tis his main hope;
15 For where there is advantage to be given,
Both more and less have given him the revolt;
And none serve with him but constrained things,
Whose hearts are absent too.

19-21 Macduff warns against overconfidence and advises that they attend to the business of fighting.

22-27 Siward says that the approaching battle will decide whether their claims will match what they actually possess (***owe***). Right now, their hopes and expectations are the product of guesswork (***thoughts speculative***); only fighting (***strokes***) can settle (***arbitrate***) the issue.

4 ***ague:*** fever.

5-7 Macbeth complains that the attackers have been reinforced (***forced***) by deserters (***those that should be ours***), which has forced him to wait at Dunsinane instead of seeking victory on the battlefield.

Macduff.   Let our just censures

20   Attend the true event, and put we on
      Industrious soldiership.

Siward.   The time approaches
      That will with due decision make us know
      What we shall say we have, and what we owe.

25   Thoughts speculative their unsure hopes relate,
      But certain issue strokes must arbitrate;
      Towards which advance the war.

[Exeunt, marching.]

Scene 5 *Dunsinane. Within the castle.*

> *Convinced of his powers, Macbeth mocks the*
> *enemy; his slaughters have left him fearless.*
> *News of Lady Macbeth's death stirs little*
> *emotion, only a comment on the emptiness of*
> *life. However, when a messenger reports that*
> *Birnam Wood seems to be moving toward the*
> *castle, Macbeth grows agitated. Fearing that*
> *the prophecies have deceived him, he decides*
> *to leave the castle to fight and die on the*
> *battlefield.*

[Enter Macbeth, Seyton, and Soldiers, with Drum and
Colors.]

Macbeth. Hang out our banners on the outward walls.
      The cry is still, "They come!" Our castle's strength
      Will laugh a siege to scorn. Here let them lie
      Till famine and the ague eat them up.

5   Were they not forced with those that should be ours,
      We might have met them dareful, beard to beard,
      And beat them backward home.

[A cry within of women.]

                                    What is that noise?

Seyton. It is the cry of women, my good lord. *[Exit.]*

10-16 There was a time when a scream in the night would have frozen Macbeth in fear and a terrifying tale (*dismal treatise*) would have made his hair (*fell*) stand on end. But since he has fed on horror (*direness*), it cannot stir (*start*) him anymore.

19-25 Macbeth wishes that his wife had died later (*hereafter*), when he would have had time to mourn her. He is moved to express despair about his own meaningless life: the future promises monotonous repetition (*Tomorrow, and tomorrow, and tomorrow*), and the past merely illustrates death's power. He wishes his life could be snuffed out like a candle.

26-30 Macbeth compares life to an actor who only briefly plays a part. Life is senseless, like a tale told by a raving idiot. *Do you feel sorry for Macbeth here?*

37 *anon:* at once.

Macbeth. I have almost forgot the taste of fears.
The time has been, my senses would have cooled
To hear a night-shriek, and my fell of hair
Would at a dismal treatise rouse and stir
As life were in't. I have supped full with horrors.
Direness, familiar to my slaughterous thoughts,
Cannot once start me.

[Enter Seyton.]

Wherefore was that cry?

Seyton. The Queen, my lord, is dead.

Macbeth. She should have died hereafter;
There would have been a time for such a word.
Tomorrow, and tomorrow, and tomorrow
Creeps in this petty pace from day to day
To the last syllable of recorded time;
And all our yesterdays have lighted fools
The way to dusty death. Out, out, brief candle!
Life's but a walking shadow, a poor player,
That struts and frets his hour upon the stage
And then is heard no more. It is a tale
Told by an idiot, full of sound and fury,
Signifying nothing.

[Enter a Messenger.]

Thou com'st to use thy tongue. Thy story quickly!

Messenger. Gracious my lord,
I should report that which I say I saw,
But know not how to do't.

Macbeth.   Well, say, sir!

Messenger. As I did stand my wa
I looked toward Birnam, and a
The wood began to move.

Macbeth.   Liar a

43-57 The messenger's news has dampened Macbeth's determination (***resolution***)***;*** Macbeth begins to fear that the witches have tricked him (***To doubt the equivocation of the fiend***). His fear that the messenger tells the truth (***avouches***) makes him decide to confront the enemy instead of staying in his castle. Weary of life, he nevertheless decides to face death and ruin (***wrack***) with his armor (***harness***) on.

1-7 Malcolm commands the troops to put down their branches (***leavy screens***) and gives the battle instructions.

re Connections

40 **Messenger.** Let me endure your wrath if't be not so.
Within this three mile may you see it coming;
I say, a moving grove.

Macbeth. If thou speak'st false,
Upon the next tree shalt thou hang alive,
45 Till famine cling thee. If thy speech be sooth,
I care not if thou dost for me as much.
I pull in resolution, and begin
To doubt the equivocation of the fiend,
That lies like truth. "Fear not, till Birnam Wood
50 Do come to Dunsinane!" and now a wood
Comes toward Dunsinane. Arm, arm, and out!
If this which he avouches does appear,
There is nor flying hence nor tarrying here.
I'gin to be aweary of the sun,
55 And wish the estate o' the world were now undone.
Ring the alarum bell! Blow wind, come wrack,
At least we'll die with harness on our back!

[Exeunt.]

Scene 6 *Dunsinane. Before the castle.*

Malcolm and the combined forces reach the castle, throw away their camouflage, and prepare for battle.

[Drum and Colors. Enter Malcolm, Siward, Macduff, and their Army, with boughs.]

Malcolm. Now near enough. Your leavy screens throw down
And show like those you are. You, worthy uncle,
Shall with my cousin, your right noble son,
5 Lead our first battle. Worthy Macduff and we
Shall take upon's what else remains to do,
According to our order.

Siward. Fare you well.

9 *power:* forces.

13 *harbingers:* announcers.

1-4 Macbeth compares himself to a bear tied to a post, a reference to the sport of bearbaiting, in which a bear was tied to a stake and attacked by dogs.

Do we but find the tyrant's power tonight,
10   Let us be beaten if we cannot fight.

Macduff. Make all our trumpets speak, give them all
        breath,
    Those clamorous harbingers of blood and death.

[Exeunt. Alarums continued.]

Scene 7 *Another part of the battlefield.*

*Macbeth kills young Siward, which restores his
belief that he cannot be killed by any man
born of a woman. Meanwhile, Macduff
searches for the hated king. Young Siward's
father reports that Macbeth's soldiers have
surrendered and that many have even joined
their attackers.*

[Enter Macbeth.]

Macbeth. They have tied me to a stake. I cannot fly,
    But bearlike I must fight the course. What's he
    That was not born of woman? Such a one
    Am I to fear, or none.

[Enter Young Siward.]

5   **Young Siward.** What is thy name?

Macbeth.   Thou'lt be afraid to hear it.

Young Siward. No; though thou call'st thyself a hotter
        name
    Than any is in hell.

10 **Macbeth.**   My name's Macbeth.

Young Siward. The devil himself could not pronounce
        a title
    More hateful to mine ear.

Macbeth.   No, nor more fearful.

18-20 *Do you think Macbeth is justified in his confidence?*

21-27 Macduff enters alone. He wants to avenge the murders of his wife and children and hopes to find Macbeth before someone else has the chance to kill him. Macduff does not want to fight the miserable hired soldiers (**kerns**), who are armed only with spears (**staves**). If he can't fight Macbeth, Macduff will leave his sword unused (**undeeded**).

27-30 After hearing sounds suggesting that a person of great distinction (**note**) is nearby, Macduff exists in pursuit of Macbeth.

31 **gently rendered:** surrendered without a fight.

34 You have almost won the day.

36-37 During the battle many of Macbeth's men deserted to Malcolm's army.

15 **Young Siward.** Thou liest, abhorred tyrant! With my
sword
I'll prove the lie thou speak'st.

[Fight, and Young Siward *slain.]*

Macbeth.   Thou wast born of woman.
But swords I smile at, weapons laugh to scorn,
20   Brandished by man that's of a woman born. *[Exit.]*

[Alarums. Enter Macduff.*]*

Macduff. That way the noise is. Tyrant, show thy face!
If thou beest slain and with no stroke of mine,
My wife and children's ghosts will haunt me still.
I cannot strike at wretched kerns, whose arms
25   Are hired to bear their staves. Either thou, Macbeth,
Or else my sword with an unbattered edge
I sheathe again undeeded. There thou shouldst be.
By this great clatter one of greatest note
Seems bruited. Let me find him, Fortune!
30   And more I beg not.

[Exit. Alarums.]

[Enter Malcolm *and* Siward.*]*

Siward. This way, my lord. The castle's gently rendered:
The tyrant's people on both sides do fight;
The noble thanes do bravely in the war;
The day almost itself professes yours,
35   And little is to do.

Malcolm.   We have met with foes
That strike beside us.

Siward.   Enter, sir, the castle.

[Exeunt. Alarum.]

1-3 Macbeth vows to continue fighting, refusing to commit suicide in the style of a defeated Roman general.

5-7 Macbeth does not want to fight Macduff, having already killed so many members of Macduff's family. *Do you think Macbeth regrets his past actions?*

11-16 Macbeth says that Macduff is wasting his effort. Trying to wound Macbeth is as useless as trying to wound the invulnerable (***intrenchant***) air. Macduff should attack other, more easily injured foes, described in terms of helmets (***crests***).

Scene 8 *Another part of the battlefield.*

Macduff finally hunts down Macbeth, who is reluctant to fight because he has already killed too many Macduffs. The still-proud Macbeth tells his enemy that no man born of a woman can defeat him, only to learn that Macduff was ripped from his mother's womb, thus not born naturally. Rather than face humiliation, Macbeth decides to fight to the death. After their fight takes them elsewhere, the Scottish lords, now in charge of Macbeth's castle, discuss young Siward's noble death. Macduff returns carrying Macbeth's bloody head, proclaiming final victory and declaring Malcolm king of Scotland. The new king thanks his supporters and promises rewards, while asking for God's help to restore order and harmony.

[Enter Macbeth.]

Macbeth. Why should I play the Roman fool and die
On mine own sword? Whiles I see lives, the gashes
Do better upon them.

[Enter Macduff.]

Macduff.   Turn, hellhound, turn!

5   **Macbeth.** Of all men else I have avoided thee.
But get thee back! My soul is too much charged
With blood of thine already.

Macduff.   I have no words;
My voice is in my sword, thou bloodier villain
10   Than terms can give thee out!

[Fight. Alarum.]

Macbeth.   Thou losest labor.
As easy mayst thou the intrenchant air
With thy keen sword impress as make me bleed.
Let fall thy blade on vulnerable crests.
15   I bear a charmed life, which must not yield
To one of woman born.

19-20 ***Macduff . . . untimely ripped:*** Macduff was a premature baby delivered by Caesarean section, an operation that removes the child directly from the mother's womb.

22 ***cowed my better part of man:*** made my spirit, or soul, fearful.

23-26 The cheating witches (***juggling fiends***) have tricked him (***palter with us***) with words that have double meanings.

27-31 Macduff scornfully tells Macbeth to surrender so that he can become a public spectacle (***the show and gaze o' the time***). Macbeth's picture will be hung on a pole (***Painted upon a pole***) as if he were part of a circus sideshow.

32-39 Macbeth cannot face the shame of surrender and public ridicule. He prefers to fight to the death (***try the last***) against Macduff, even though he knows all hope is gone. *What is your opinion of Macbeth's attitude?*

The first trumpet call (***Retreat***) signals the battle's end. The next one (***flourish***) announces Malcolm's entrance.

41-42 Though some must die (***go off***) in battle, Siward can see that their side does not have many casualties.

Macduff.   Despair thy charm!
And let the angel whom thou still hast served
Tell thee, Macduff was from his mother's womb
20   Untimely ripped.

Macbeth. Accursed be that tongue that tells me so,
For it hath cowed my better part of man!
And be these juggling fiends no more believed,
That palter with us in a double sense,
25   That keep the word of promise to our ear
And break it to our hope! I'll not fight with thee!

Macduff. Then yield thee, coward,
And live to be the show and gaze o' the time!
We'll have thee, as our rarer monsters are,
30   Painted upon a pole, and underwrit
"Here may you see the tyrant."

Macbeth.   I will not yield,
To kiss the ground before young Malcolm's feet
And to be baited with the rabble's curse.
35   Though Birnam Wood be come to Dunsinane,
And thou opposed, being of no woman born,
Yet I will try the last. Before my body
I throw my warlike shield. Lay on, Macduff,
And damned be him that first cries "Hold, enough!"

[Exeunt fighting. Alarums.]

[Retreat and flourish. Enter, with Drum and Colors, Malcolm,
Siward, Ross, Thanes, *and* Soldiers.*]*

40   **Malcolm.** I would the friends we miss were safe arrived.

Siward. Some must go off; and yet, by these I see,
So great a day as this is cheaply bought.

Malcolm. Macduff is missing, and your noble son.

Ross. Your son, my lord, has paid a soldier's debt.

50-52 Ross tells old Siward that if he mourns his son according to the boy's value, his sorrow will never end.

53 *hurts before:* wounds on the front of his body, which would give further evidence of his courage.

58 *knell is knolled:* Young Siward's death bell has already rung, meaning there is no need to mourn him further. *What do you think of old Siward's refusal to grieve for his son?*

Macduff is probably carrying Macbeth's head on a pole.

65-66 *The time . . . pearl:* Macduff declares that the age (*time*) is now freed from tyranny. He sees Malcolm surrounded by Scotland's noblest men (*thy kingdom's pearl*).

71-86 Malcolm promises that he will quickly reward his nobles according to the devotion (*several loves*) they have shown. He gives the thanes new titles (*Henceforth be Earls*) and declares his intention, as a sign of the new age (*planted newly with the time*), to welcome back the exiles who fled Macbeth's tyranny and his cruel agents (*ministers*). Now that Scotland is free of the butcher Macbeth and his queen, who is reported to have killed herself, Malcolm asks for God's help to restore order and harmony. He concludes by inviting all present to his coronation.

45 He only lived but till he was a man,
The which no sooner had his prowess confirmed
In the unshrinking station where he fought
But like a man he died.

Siward. Then he is dead?

50 **Ross.** Ay, and brought off the field. Your cause of sorrow
Must not be measured by his worth, for then
It hath no end.

Siward. Had he his hurts before?

Ross. Ay, on the front.

55 **Siward.** Why then, God's soldier be he!
Had I as many sons as I have hairs,
I would not wish them to a fairer death.
And so his knell is knolled.

Malcolm. He's worth more sorrow,
60 And that I'll spend for him.

Siward. He's worth no more.
They say he parted well and paid his score,
And so, God be with him! Here comes newer comfort.

[Enter Macduff, *with* Macbeth's *head.]*

Macduff. Hail, King! for so thou art. Behold where stands
65 The usurper's cursed head. The time is free.
I see thee compassed with thy kingdom's pearl,
That speak my salutation in their minds;
Whose voices I desire aloud with mine—
Hail, King of Scotland!

70 **All.** Hail, King of Scotland! *[Flourish.]*

Malcolm. We shall not spend a large expense of time
Before we reckon with your several loves
And make us even with you. My Thanes and kinsmen,
Henceforth be Earls, the first that ever Scotland

75　In such an honor named. What's more to do
　　Which would be planted newly with the time—
　　As calling home our exiled friends abroad
　　That fled the snares of watchful tyranny,
　　Producing forth the cruel ministers
80　Of this dead butcher and his fiendlike queen,
　　Who (as 'tis thought) by self and violent hands
　　Took off her life—this, and what needful else
　　That calls upon us, by the grace of Grace
　　We will perform in measure, time, and place.
85　So thanks to all at once and to each one,
　　Whom we invite to see us crowned at Scone.

[Flourish. Exeunt omnes.]

RELATED READINGS

Insomniac

by Octavio Paz

Macbeth is filled with characters who find it hard to sleep at night, either because they have evil deeds to perform, because they are haunted by guilt from having performed the deeds, or simply because the atmosphere is charged with impending evil. The speaker in the following poem sounds as though he or she stepped out of Macbeth to reflect on yet another sleepless night.

Nightwatch of the mirror:
the moon keeps it company.
Reflection on reflection,
the spider spins its plots.

5   Hardly ever blinking,
thoughts are on guard:
neither ghost nor concept,
my death is a sentry.

Not alive, not dead:
10 awake, I am awake
in the desert of an eye.

Better Than Counting Sheep

by Robert Penn Warren

*When do you find it hard to sleep and what
is your remedy for a sleepless night? The
following poem might be amusing advice
for the sleepless Macbeth household.*

For a night when sleep eludes you, I have,
At last, found the formula. Try to summon

All those ever known who are dead now, and
    soon
It will seem they are there in your room, not
    chairs enough

5   For the party, or standing space even, the hall
Chock-full, and faces thrust to the pane to
    peer.

Then somehow the house, in a wink, isn't
    there,
But a field full of folk, and some,

Those near, touch your sleeve, so sadly and
    slow, and all
10   Want something of you, too timid to
    ask—and you don't

Know what. Yes, even in distance and
    dimness, hands
Are out-stretched to glow faintly

Like fox-fire in marshland where deadfall
Rots, though a few trunks unsteadily stand.

15   Meanwhile, in the grieving susurrus, all
      wordless,
You sense, at last, what they want. Each,

Male or female, young or age-gnawed,
    beloved or not—
Each wants to know if you remember a
    name.

But now you can't answer, not even your
    mother's name, and your heart
20   Howls with the loneliness of a wolf in

The depth of a snow-throttled forest when
    the moon, full,
Spills the spruce-shadows African black.
    Then you are, suddenly,

Alone. And your own name gone, as you
    plunge in ink-shadow or snowdrift.
The shadows are dreams—but of what? And
    the snowdrift, sleep.

Macbeth

by Norrie Epstein

Some people respond to Shakespeare by writing critical essays about his works. The following essay explores several aspects of Macbeth: *how the boundaries between good and evil become hopelessly blurred in this gloomy setting; whether the witches' statement that Macbeth will be king is a warning, a temptation, or a prophecy; and whether Macbeth is a criminal or a tragic hero.*

Macbeth is visually dark, a Shakespearean *film noir*. There's only one moment of sunlight, just before Duncan's murder. The rest of the play takes place in shadows, in rain, in storms, at twilight, or in the middle of the night. Because the play is so short, it's dense with the intensity of a fever dream, filled with prophecies, ghosts, daggers hovering in midair, shrieks in the night pitched ever more shrill by a deepening paranoia and dread. Although the story of Macbeth *is* as exciting as a murder mystery, it's the play's atmosphere, not its plot, that's the thing. For gloomy intensity, there's nothing like it in all of Shakespeare.

The play opens on a "blasted heath," where the air is so filthy and foggy (like the smoky streets of Los Angeles in a classic *film noir)* that one can barely see. Visual obscurity here suggests moral ambiguity, the boundaries between good and evil incomprehensibly blurred. *Macbeth* depicts a disorienting world where "Fair is foul, and foul is fair." Upon entering this blasted heath, we, along with Macbeth, leave moral guideposts behind us.

Here the three Weird Sisters, like mysterious

strangers lurking in a dark alley, wait to give the hero a tip about a future event. For at this point, Macbeth *is* still a hero, fresh from the battlefield where his valor led to victory. As he passes, the Witches greet him with a repetition of three pronouncements (three being a magical number). The first Witch presents him with a known truth:

All hail, Macbeth! Hail to thee, Thane of Glamis!

The next, with a possibility that will become true:

All hail, Macbeth! Hail to thee, Thane of Cawdor!

And the last, with a statement that's seemingly beyond his grasp:

All hail, Macbeth, that shalt be king hereafter!

Thus, by degrees, they lead him from the actual to the probable and then, finally, to the seemingly impossible. Upon hearing the final pronouncement, Macbeth's hair becomes "unfix[ed]" and "[his] seated heart knock[s] at [his] ribs."

The central question of the play is whether the Witch's final statement is a warning, a temptation, or a prophecy. The mystery is not, as the woman in Thurber's story thought, a whodunit, but a whocausedit? What role do the Weird Sisters play in Macbeth's fate? "*Wyrd*" meant "fate" in Anglo-Saxon. But the word, as the critic Marvin Rosenburg points out, also suggests "weyward," or "wayward," the Witches being projections of Macbeth's wayward imagination. Do they determine his fate or merely suggest what his ambition craves? Shakespeare thus asks, Are our lives determined by fate or by free will?

The prophecy arouses complex emotions in Lady

Macbeth. She is frequently called ambitious, but her aspirations are fired by an intense sexual current. She's concerned not with Macbeth as her husband but with her husband as king. She is compelled by male power, and by appealing to her husband's manhood, she seduces and humiliates him into doing a deed that at first he only contemplates:

> **Macbeth.** I dare do all that may become a man;
>   Who dares do more is none.
> **Lady.** What beast was't then
>   That made you break this enterprise to me?
>   When you durst do it, then you were a man;
>   And to be more than what you were, you would
>   Be so much more the man.

> *(I.7.46—51)*

By murdering Duncan, Macbeth violates and disrupts divine, human, and natural laws: he has murdered his king, to whom he owes complete loyalty; his kinsman, whom he should love; and his guest, who deserves his hospitality and protection. And he has killed an innocent man while he lies asleep and defenseless. Most important, Duncan is a wise and a good ruler. Unlike Bolingbroke in *Richard II,* Macbeth has no political or moral excuse for his deed. All of nature revolts against Duncan's murder. By killing the king, who presides over earthly order, Macbeth sets off a chain reaction that unleashes anarchy in heaven and on earth: the eve of Duncan's murder is "unruly" (i.e., unruled); a violent storm suddenly picks up; the earth shakes as if with a fever; Duncan's horses turn wild and eat each other; and prophetic shrieks fill the night air.

After Duncan's murder, Shakespeare creates one of the most harrowing scenes imaginable. Husband and wife, now accomplices, speak in a terse, conspiratorial whisper, the atmosphere one of suppressed hysteria. If they weren't whispering, they'd be screaming.

> **Macbeth.** I have done the deed. Didst thou not
>   hear a noise?
> **Lady.** I heard the owl-scream and the cricket's
>   cry. Did not you speak?
> **Macbeth.**   When?
> **Lady.**   Now.
> **Macbeth.**   As I descended?
> **Lady.** Ay.

(II.2.14—16)

Their nerves are so raw, every noise seems like an explosion. Staring at his bloody hands, Macbeth at last recognizes that the murder is no longer an abstract idea but an accomplished fact. "To know my deed 'twere best not know myself." This one act has transformed him, irrevocably, from Macbeth into an assassin, strange to himself. But Lady Macbeth dismisses such talk as childish: "A little water clears us of this deed." Yet Macbeth soon becomes accustomed to his new identity. He has killed to get the throne, and his reign becomes one long bloodbath in a futile attempt to maintain it.

As in most *film noir,* the distinction between criminal and hero is vague. For a while, Macbeth still has a conscience. He broods on the deed; he can't sleep; Banquo's ghost appears to him; and he's filled with dread at what he has become. A decent man imprisoned in a murderer's body, he can only stand back and watch as the killer continues to strike. The play's real terror comes not from Macbeth's deeds but from how they transform and corrupt him. Shakespeare was one of the first writers to create both criminal and hero in the same person. He penetrates into what Joseph Conrad would later call the "heart of darkness"—the potential for evil within every civilized human being. If the honorable Macbeth could kill his king, then anything is possible—on heaven, on earth, and within the heart of man.

Macbeth briefly enjoys a sense of security as the stereotypical hardboiled villain—after all, he is now king, the Witches have assured him of his continued success, and his only threat comes from two seemingly unnatural occurrences: from a man not "of woman born" and when Birnam Wood marches to Dunsinane. In his eagerness to feel secure, Macbeth forgets that the Witches are crafty equivocators who play with words, making truth seem like fiction and fiction, truth.

Guilt or Indigestion?

In an article on the Scottish national dish, haggis, the *Newsweek* writer Mark Starr wrote, "A number of Shakespearean revisionists now believe that Macbeth spied the ghost of Banquo at the banquet not out of guilt, but as a result of having just dined on haggis." Starr helpfully provides the recipe: "Sheep's lungs, heart and liver, mixed with suet, oats and seasonings—all boiled in the animal's stomach."

Even as Macduff and the English forces gather around him, Macbeth struggles to maintain his sense of invulnerability. But as events start closing in and he becomes increasingly isolated, his beliefs topple, one by one, as he sees through the illusion of worldly power. Kingship, power, his wife,

Louis Marder cites a German production of the play in which in each act, the walls of the stage increasingly close in on Macbeth.

existence itself are meaningless. Macbeth is one of the first existentialist antiheroes. Inured to horror, he is exhausted, bored, and cruel. After basing his existence on portents and prophecies, he now looks at life and sees that tomorrow is just as meaningless as today:

> Tomorrow, and tomorrow, and tomorrow,
> Creeps in this petty pace from day to day
> To the last syllable of recorded time;
> And all our yesterdays have lighted fools
> The way to dusty death. Out, out, brief candle!
> Life's but a walking shadow, a poor player
> That struts and frets his hour upon the stage
> And then is heard no more. It is a tale
> Told by an idiot, full of sound and fury,
> Signifying nothing.
>
> *(V.5.19—28)*

As he wades through evil, Macbeth moves further and further away from all natural human impulses and sensations. The murder that first bound him to his wife has now driven them apart. Once, Lady Macbeth believed that "a little water" could wash her of the deed; now she compulsively washes her hands, unable to rid herself of guilt. Horrified by her capacity for sin, she relives the crime over and over again. Upon learning that Lady Macbeth, the sole prop of his life, has committed suicide, Macbeth says, "She should have died hereafter."

The story of a bad man who commits a crime is not a tragedy but a straightforward tale of evil. *Macbeth*, however, is about a good man who becomes evil, and that is his tragedy. At the end, numb to all feeling, he distantly remembers what he once was and what it was like to be human:

I have almost forgot the taste of fears.
The time has been my senses would have cooled
To hear a night-shriek, and my fell of hair
Would at a dismal treatise rouse and stir
As life were in't. I have supped full with horrors:
Direness, familiar to my slaughterous thoughts,
Cannot once start me.

(V.5.9—15)

It is his capacity for self-scrutiny that makes Macbeth a worthy tragic subject. He never lies to himself about the nature of his deed, never rationalizes to justify his actions. Aware that he is doomed, he pursues his damnation headlong to his own destruction.

Like a Bad Dream

by Heinrich Böll,
translated by Leila Vennewitz

*In her first speech, Lady Macbeth
complains about Macbeth's reluctance to
do whatever is necessary to get ahead in
life. The following story shows another
ambitious woman who teaches her
husband about getting ahead through the
art of making deals.*

That evening we had invited the Zumpens over for
dinner, nice people; it was through my father-in-law
that we had got to know them: ever since we have
been married he has helped me to meet people who
can be useful to me in business, and Zumpen can be
useful: he is chairman of a committee which places
contracts for large housing projects, and I have
married into the excavating business.

I was tense that evening, but Bertha, my wife,
reassured me. "The fact," she said, "that he's coming
at all is promising. Just try and get the conversation
round to the contract. You know it's tomorrow
they're going to be awarded."

I stood looking through the net curtains of the glass
front door, waiting for Zumpen. I smoked, ground the
cigarette butts under my foot, and shoved them under
the mat. Next I took up a position at the bathroom
window and stood there wondering why Zumpen had
accepted the invitation; he couldn't be that interested
in having dinner with us, and the fact that the big
contract I was involved in was going to be awarded
tomorrow must have made the whole thing as
embarrassing to him as it was to me.

I thought about the contract too: it was a big one, I would make 20,000 marks on the deal, and I wanted the money.

Bertha had decided what I was to wear: a dark jacket, trousers a shade lighter and a conservative tie. That's the kind of thing she learned at home, and at boarding school from the nuns. Also what to offer guests: when to pass the cognac, and when the vermouth, how to arrange dessert. It is comforting to have a wife who knows all about such things.

But Bertha was tense too: as she put her hands on my shoulders, they touched my neck, and I felt her thumbs damp and cold against it.

"It's going to be all right," she said, "You'll get the contract."

"Christ," I said, "it means 20,000 marks to me, and you know how we need the money."

"One should never," she said gently, "mention Christ's name in connection with money!"

A dark car drew up in front of our house, a make I didn't recognize, but it looked Italian. "Take it easy," Bertha whispered, "wait till they've rung, let them stand there for a couple of seconds, then walk slowly to the door and open it."

I watched Mr. and Mrs. Zumpen come up the steps: he is slender and tall, with graying temples, the kind of man who fifty years ago would have been known as a "ladies' man"; Mrs. Zumpen is one of those thin dark women who always make me think of lemons. I could tell from Zumpen's face that it was a frightful bore for him to have dinner with us.

Then the doorbell rang, and I waited one second, two seconds, walked slowly to the door and opened it.

"Well," I said, "how nice of you to come!"

Cognac glasses in hand, we went from room to room in our apartment, which the Zumpens wanted to see. Bertha stayed in the kitchen to squeeze some mayonnaise out of a tube onto the appetizers; she does this very nicely: hearts, loops, little houses. The Zumpens complimented us on our apartment; thcy exchanged smiles when they saw the big desk in my study, at that moment it seemed a bit too big even to me.

Zumpen admired a small rococo cabinet, a wedding present from my grandmother, and a baroque Madonna in our bedroom.

By the time we got back to the dining room, Bertha had dinner on the table; she had done this very nicely too, it was all so attractive yet so natural, and dinner was pleasant and relaxed. We talked about movies and books, about the recent elections, and Zumpen praised the assortment of cheeses, and Mrs. Zumpen praised the coffee and the pastries. Then we showed the Zumpens our honeymoon pictures: photographs of the Breton coast, Spanish donkeys, and street scenes from Casablanca.

After that we had some more cognac, and when I stood up to get the box with the photos of the time when we were engaged, Bertha gave me a sign, and I didn't get the box. For two minutes there was absolute silence, because we had nothing more to talk about, and we all thought about the contract; I thought of the 20,000 marks, and it struck me that I could deduct the bottle of cognac from my income tax. Zumpen looked at his watch and said: "Too bad, it's ten o'clock; we have to go. It's been such a pleasant evening!" And Mrs. Zumpen said: "It was really delightful, and I hope you'll come to us one evening."

"We would love to," Bertha said, and we stood around for another half-minute, all thinking again about the contract, and I felt Zumpen was waiting for me to take him aside and bring up the subject. But I didn't. Zumpen kissed Bertha's hand, and I went ahead, opened the doors, and held the car door open for Mrs. Zumpen down below.

"Why," said Bertha gently, "didn't you mention the contract to him? You know it's going to be awarded tomorrow."

"Well," I said, "I didn't know how to bring the conversation round to it."

"Now look," she said in a quiet voice, "you could have used any excuse to ask him into your study, that's where you should have talked to him. You must have noticed how interested he is in art. You ought to have said: I have an eighteenth-century crucifix in there you might like to have a look at, and then . . . "

I said nothing, and she sighed and tied on her apron. I followed her into the kitchen; we put the rest of the appetizers back in the refrigerator, and I crawled about on the floor looking for the top of the mayonnaise tube. I put away the remains of the cognac, counted the cigars: Zumpen had smoked only one. I emptied the ashtrays, ate another pastry, and looked to see if there was any coffee left in the pot. When I went back to the kitchen, Bertha was standing there with the car key in her hand.

"What's up?" I asked.

"We have to go over there, of course," she said.

"Over where?"

"To the Zumpens," she said, "where do you think?"

"It's nearly half past ten."

"I don't care if it's midnight," Bertha said, "all I know is, there's 20,000 marks involved. Don't imagine they're squeamish."

She went into the bathroom to get ready, and I stood behind her watching her wipe her mouth and draw in new outlines, and for the first time I noticed how wide and primitive that mouth is. When she tightened the knot of my tie I could have kissed her, the way I always used to when she fixed my tie, but I didn't.

Downtown the cafés and restaurants were brightly lit. People were sitting outside on the terraces, and the light from the street lamps was caught in the silver ice-cream dishes and ice buckets. Bertha gave me an encouraging look; but she stayed in the car when we stopped in front of the Zumpens' house, and I pressed the bell at once and was surprised how quickly the door was opened. Mrs. Zumpen did not seem surprised to see me; she had on some black lounging pajamas with loose full trousers embroidered with yellow flowers, and this made me think more than ever of lemons.

"I beg your pardon," I said, "I would like to speak to your husband."

"He's gone out again," she said, "he'll be back in half an hour."

In the hall I saw a lot of Madonnas, gothic and baroque, even rococo Madonnas, if there is such a thing.

"I see," I said, "well then, if you don't mind, I'll come back in half an hour."

Bertha had bought an evening paper; she was reading it and smoking, and when I sat down beside her she said: "I think you could have talked about it to her too."

"But how do you know he wasn't there?"

"Because I know he is at the Gaffel Club playing chess, as he does every Wednesday evening at this time."

"You might have told me that earlier."

"Please try and understand," said Bertha, folding the newspaper. "I am trying to help you, I want you to find out for yourself how to deal with such things. All we had to do was call up Father and he would have settled the whole thing for you with one phone call, but I want you to get the contract on your own."

"All right," I said, "then what'll we do: wait here

half an hour, or go up right away and have a talk with her?"

"We'd better go up right away," said Bertha.

We got out of the car and went up in the elevator together. "Life," said Bertha, "consists of making compromises and concessions."

Mrs. Zumpen was no more surprised now than she had been earlier, when I had come alone. She greeted us, and we followed her into her husband's study. Mrs. Zumpen brought some cognac, poured it out, and before I could say anything about the contract she pushed a yellow folder toward me: "Housing Project Fir Tree Haven," I read, and looked up in alarm at Mrs. Zumpen, at Bertha, but they both smiled, and Mrs. Zumpen said: "Open the folder," and I opened it; inside was another one, pink, and on this I read: "Housing Project Fir Tree Haven—Excavation Work." I opened this too, saw my estimate lying there on top of the pile; along the upper edge someone had written in red: "Lowest bid."

I could feel myself flushing with pleasure, my heart thumping, and I thought of the 20,000 marks.

"Christ," I said softly, and closed the file, and this time Bertha forgot to rebuke me.

"*Prost,*" said Mrs. Zumpen with a smile, "let's drink to it then."

We drank, and I stood up and said: "It may seem rude of me, but perhaps you'll understand that I would like to go home now."

"I understand perfectly," said Mrs. Zumpen, "there's just one small item to be taken care of." She took the file, leafed through it, and said: "Your price per square meter is thirty pfennigs below that of the next-lowest bidder. I suggest you raise your price by fifteen pfennigs: that way you'll still be the lowest and you'll have made an extra four thousand five hundred marks. Come on, do it now!" Bertha took her pen out of her purse and offered it to me, but I was in too much of a turmoil to write; I gave the file to Bertha and watched her alter the price with a steady hand, rewrite the total, and hand the file back to Mrs. Zumpen.

"And now," said Mrs. Zumpen, "just one more little thing. Get out your check book and write a check for three thousand marks; it must be a cash check and endorsed by you."

She had said this to me, but it was Bertha who pulled our check book out of her purse and made out the check.

"It won't be covered," I said in a low voice.

"When the contract is awarded, there will be an advance, and then it will be covered," said Mrs. Zumpen.

Perhaps I failed to grasp what was happening at the time. As we went down in the elevator, Bertha said she was happy, but I said nothing.

Bertha chose a different way home, we drove through quiet residential districts, I saw lights in open windows, people sitting on balconies drinking wine; it was a clear, warm night.

"I suppose the check was for Zumpen?" was all I said, softly, and Bertha replied, just as softly: "Of course."

I looked at Bertha's small, brown hands on the steering wheel, so confident and quiet. Hands, I thought, that sign checks and squeeze mayonnaise tubes, and I looked higher—at her mouth, and still felt no desire to kiss it.

That evening I did not help Bertha put the car away in the garage, nor did I help her with the dishes. I poured myself a large cognac, went up to my study, and sat down at my desk, which was much too big for me. I was wondering about something. I got up, went into the bedroom and looked at the baroque

Madonna, but even there I couldn't put my finger on the thing I was wondering about.

The ringing of the phone interrupted my thoughts; I lifted the receiver and was not surprised to hear Zumpen's voice.

"Your wife," he said, "made a slight mistake. She raised the price by twenty-five pfennigs instead of fifteen."

I thought for a moment and then said: "That wasn't a mistake, she did it with my consent."

He was silent for a second or two, then said with a laugh: "So you had already discussed the various possibilities?"

"Yes," I said.

"All right, then make out another check for a thousand."

"Five hundred," I said, and I thought: It's like a bad dream—that's what it's like.

"Eight hundred," he said, and I said with a laugh: "Six hundred," and I knew, although I had no experience to go on, that he would now say seven hundred and fifty, and when he did I said "Yes" and hung up.

It was not yet midnight when I went downstairs and over to the car to give Zumpen the check; he was alone and laughed as I reached in to hand him the folded check. When I walked slowly back into the house, there was no sign of Bertha; she didn't appear when I went back into my study; she didn't appear when I went downstairs again for a glass of milk from the refrigerator, and I knew what she was thinking; she was thinking: he has to get over it, and I have to leave him alone; this is something he has to understand.

But I never did understand. It is beyond understanding.

How Many Children Had Lady Macbeth?

by Don Nigro

Many actors have claimed that Macbeth *is a cursed play. In this monologue, a woman describes how her ambition to play the role of Lady Macbeth has led to some funny and also some sad consequences.*

(There is one character, BONNIE, a pretty young woman of thirty, barefoot, wearing a leotard and bluejeans, on a bare stage with just one high stool. As she begins to speak to us, she will take off the bluejeans and begin to do gentle actor's stretches and warmups while she talks, using the floor and the stool. As she gets more involved in her story, she will warm up less, and by the last part she will be sitting on the stool, just talking to us.)

Bonnie. Actors have always known the Scottish play is haunted, and some of them have very definite rules about it—you must never quote it backstage, and if you must refer to it, you never say its title, you call it the Scottish play, or sometimes even a *certain* Scottish play. And this curse that's on it is supposed to account for the great number of perfectly dreadful productions of it, although in fact most productions of most plays are pretty dreadful, when you come right down to it, especially of Shakespeare. There is, you see, an unspoken mythology perpetrated by crummy directors and producers who think people are stupid so plays should also be stupid, that the easier a play is to put on adequately, the better the play is, which, if it were true, would make *Barefoot in the Park* a much better play than *King Lear*. I think it's this cretinous myth that's led modern playwrights to allow directors and producers to coax, harass, cajole, threaten and intimidate them into hacking away whatever is most brave and subtle and complex and different and interesting in their work, leaving finally only a kind of oatmeal the director feels less threatened by—the rule seems to be, if we can't make it work in the first rehearsal, it's the play's fault, cut it, when of course anybody who's worked on Shakespeare or Chekhov or for that matter anything of value knows that it's usually those things that worked so well in the first rehearsal that have grown so stale and dead by the week before opening that they have to be redone anyway, while those very parts of the play that seemed most impossible early on, that you had to bang your head against again and again, screaming and swearing and crying and getting you horribly frustrated until in a fit of despair or out of utter exhaustion an entirely different reading from somewhere suddenly flows out of you, and it's not at all what you expected but it works and turns out to be the best moment in the production. But with new plays this seldom gets a chance to happen, because the best parts get cut in rehearsal, and that's part of the reason most contemporary drama really sucks, that and greed and a lot of other things I don't want to talk about right now because I don't want to get too angry, I've got to go be Mariana in the moated grange this evening—*Measure for Measure,* one of Willy's secret best. Not such a great part, though, but I don't care, I'll do Shakespeare any time, any where, to my agent's increasing fury and at the expense of a great many long-running national dog food and deodorant commercials I might have lived quite comfortably on. I've done four Mirandas, three

Cordelias, I just did Ophelia in New Jersey, but my favorite play, for some reason, has always been the Scottish play, and the role I always wanted was Lady Mac.

I'd been in other productions of it, playing various kinds of female set decoration, an attending gentlewoman, a very young and more or less naked witch, and I must confess to you, all of these productions were major or minor disasters of one sort or another. People got whacked or mauled in the fight scenes, lights fell near people's heads, there were two bomb threats, one of which, the one where I was the naked young witch, I'm convinced was called in by Shakespeare himself. My favorite bad production of my favorite play was the one in which a certain attendant Lord was to carry on the dead body of Lady Mac just as the words were spoken, The Queen, my Lord, is dead. Well, this particular Lady Mac was an ex-movie star who'd put on quite a bit of weight— Lady Big Mac, we called her—they always come back to their roots in the theatre when they get too fat for the camera—and the big strong fellow whose job was to carry her dead body onstage had stepped off a platform in the dark and broken his ankle shortly before his entrance, and the only other actor available on the spur of the moment was a rather little fellow, but very macho, who insisted he could do it, no problem. So he hoisted the Amazon Lady M into his arms and staggered onstage just as the cue line, The Queen, my Lord, is dead, was spoken, lost his balance, and fell over backwards with the poor dead Queen on top of him. Well, the audience lost it, and then Macbeth lost it, and ended up giggling his way through his Tomorrow and tomorrow speech, and, well, on the whole, high tragedy it was not.

I was in another production in which one of the witches fainted from the heat in the middle of her scene and fell head first into the cauldron, and another in which a drunk in the alley behind the theatre kept playing a terrible version of *Tea for Two* on an accordion as loudly as possible during the sleepwalking scene. This was the same production where poor MacDuff developed a mental block about a rather familiar Shakespearean phrase, and every night, when learning of the murder of his wife and children burst out with

What, all my pretty chickens and their dam, in one swell foop?

But despite all this, I continued to love the play, and still longed desperately to play Lady Mac, although for a long time my ingenue looks kept me from even being considered for it. Finally, I got the chance. I was understudying a much older woman, who obligingly ran into a door backstage just before curtain and broke her nose—I was nowhere near her at the time, I swear—and so I had to go on in her place. It seemed like fate. I knew I was going to be terrific. I felt that I understood this character, everything about her, her ambition—I'm an actress, God knows I understand that—her frustration—same there—her impatience with her husband—I was married to a nice man who wanted me to quit acting and stay home and have babies, and when he finally realized I was never going to stop and take time for that, he was gone. I had dared things, I had fought, I had sacrificed, I had endured, and now, finally, I was getting my chance to play her. It was destiny. And it went very well, I mean, extremely well—I'd been waiting all my life to play this role, and the audience, which had at first been disappointed it was me, began to realize they were seeing something special, and their resentment began to turn into appreciation, they were with the play, they were lost in it, I could feel them rooting for me, they were with me, it was the best performance of our run, the old respected dull hag of a Lady M had been transformed unexpectedly into a hot and sexy younger version, that is, me, and I played the sensuality for all it was worth, and an odd kind of innocence, and humor, my Lady M had a sense of humor, and pathos, but she was hard as nails, but she had this tenderness, it was working, everything was working, the magic was there, the gods were present, old Will was beaming at us, Macbeth was actually paying attention to his wife for once, it was flowing, it was stunning, and then came the sleepwalking scene, oh, it was going so well, it was going so well, until the moron playing the Doctor, who had had a couple of drinks before the show, and seemed hypnotized by my boobs, tripped and knocked the candle over and set my nightgown on fire.

I decided to try and play it, use it, pretend we had planned it that way, it was part of the madness, see, and the girl playing the gentlewoman was quick enough to grab the bucket we had onstage, in which I was trying to wash the bloodstains off my hands, and throw it on me. The bloodstains were imaginary, but, fortunately the water was not, the bucket was nearly full, for some reason, and I was soaked, but, dammit, this was my moment, I wasn't going to let it slip away for anything, and the audience was so into it, I think they would have bought it, considered it a bit of daring technical tour de force on the director's part— I looked like the winner of a wet nightgown contest, and that alone might have kept them watching and wanting to believe, if only the gung ho assistant stage manager, who had the hots for me and was about three times too hyper for his job anyway, had not then run out onto the stage, yelled for everybody not to panic, and fire extinguished me.

I don't know. Maybe we should have gone with *Barefoot in the Park*. I built my whole life towards a moment when I was set on fire, drenched and then covered in foam in front of six hundred people. Sometimes acting is like being punished for a crime you didn't commit. Oh, well. I'll get another chance, some day. They usually cast her much too old, so I'll get a turn or two in middle age. The problem is, I've been having this odd fantasy lately. I see my children watching me play Lady Macbeth. I want my children to see me do it. Isn't that crazy? I don't have any children. And as the years go by, it becomes increasingly unlikely that I ever will, and I miss them. I miss my children. I feel like I ran off with Shakespeare and abandoned them. You make choices and then there are consequences, and then the consequences have consequences, and for a long time you don't notice this happening, because you're young and busy and have things to do and things you want and no time to stop and think about it, but the consequences just keep happening, every moment of your life has a consequence, somewhere down the line. She didn't really understand that when she made him kill the king. But consequences don't care if you understand them or not, they just keep happening, tomorrow and tomorrow, to the last syllable of recorded time. Shakespeare knew. That son of a bitch knew everything. He had children.

Poor babies. I wrote them out of my play. All my pretty ones. In one swell foop. I guess it's a curse.

(The light fades on her and goes out.)

Into Concrete Mixer Throw

by Barbara Roe

Why do you think that the witches in
Macbeth *are some of the most popular
characters Shakespeare created? In this
parody of the beginning of Act 4, Scene 1,
witches are also stirring up a magical stew
to bring trouble to humanity. Think about
the ingredients in this modern brew and
how it could affect life on this planet.*

Into concrete mixer throw
Brick from shoddy bungalow,
Thrice three chunks of orange peel
Gathered from the beach at Deal,
5   Foot of hare untimely slain
On the outer traffic lane,
Cast-off paper from a toffee,
Cup of instantaneous coffee,
Then, with fag-end torn from lip,
10   Sexy film and comic strip,
Nucleus of hydrogen,
Thousandth egg of battery hen,
Paint-brush used for marking wall,
Thoroughly compound them all.
15   This charm, once set and left to stand,
Will cast a blight on any land.

Lady Macbeth's Trouble

Letter from Lady Macbeth to Lady Macduff

by Maurice Baring

How would you explain Macbeth's behavior to one of his intended victims? In this fictional letter addressed to Lady Macduff, Lady Macbeth sounds like a concerned housewife who wants to prevent rumors from being spread about her sensitive husband.

Most Private.

The Palace, Forres,
October 10.

My dearest Flora,

I am sending this letter by Ross, who is starting for Fife to-morrow morning. I wonder if you could possibly come here for a few days. You would bring Jeamie, of course. Macbeth is devoted to children. I think we could make you quite comfortable, although of course palaces are never very comfortable, and it's all so different from dear Inverness. And there is the tiresome Court etiquette and the people, especially the Heads of the Clans, who are so touchy, and insist on one's observing every tradition. For instance, the bagpipes begin in the early morning; the pipers walk round the castle a little after sunrise, and this I find very trying, as you know what a bad sleeper I am. Only two nights ago I nearly fell out of the window walking in my sleep. The doctor, who I must say is a charming man (he was the late King's doctor, and King Duncan always used to say he was the only man who really understood his constitution), is giving me mandragora mixed with poppy and syrup; but so far it has not done me any good; but then I always was a wretched sleeper and now I am worse, because—well, I am coming at last to what I really want to say.

I am in very great trouble and I beg you to come here if you can, because you would be the greatest help. You shall have a bedroom facing south, and Jeamie shall be next to you, and my maid can look after you both, and as Macduff is going to England I think it would really be wiser and *safer* for you to come here than to stay all alone in that lonely castle of yours in these troublesome times, when there are so many robbers about and one never knows what may not happen.

I confess I have been very much put about lately. (You quite understand if you come we shall have plenty of opportunities of seeing each other alone in spite of all the tiresome etiquette and ceremonies, and of course you must treat me just the same as before; only in *public* you must just throw in a "Majesty" now and then and curtchey and call me "Ma'am" so as not to shock the people.) I am sorry to say Macbeth is not at all in good case. He is really not at all well, and the fact is he has never got over the terrible tragedy that happened at Inverness. At first I thought it was quite natural he should be upset. Of course very few people know how fond he was of his cousin. King Duncan was his favourite cousin. They had travelled together in England, and they were much more like brothers than cousins, although the King was so much older than he is. I shall never forget the evening when the King arrived after the battle against those horrid Norwegians. I was very nervous as it was, after having gone through all the anxiety of knowing that Macbeth was in danger. Then on the top of that, just after I heard that he was alive and well, the messenger arrived telling me that the King was on his way to Inverness. Of course I had got nothing ready, and Elspeth our housekeeper put on a face as much as to say that we could not possibly manage in the time. However, I said she *must* manage. I knew our cousin wouldn't expect too much, and I spent the whole day making those drop scones he used to be so fond of.

I was already worried then because Macbeth, who is superstitious, said he had met three witches on the way (he said something about it in his letter) and they had apparently been uncivil to him. I thought they were gipsies and that he had not crossed their palm with silver, but when he arrived he was still brooding over this, and was quite *odd* in his way of speaking about it. I didn't think much of this at the time, as I put it down to the strain of what he had gone through, and the reaction, which must always be great after such a time; but now it all comes back to me, and now that I think over it in view of what has happened since, I cannot help owning to myself that he was not himself, and if I had not known what a sober man he was, I should almost have thought the 1030 (Hildebrand) whisky had gone to his head—because when he talked of the old women he was quite incoherent: just like a man who has had an hallucination. But I did not think of all this till afterwards, as I put it down to the strain, as I have just told you.

But now! Well, I must go back a little way so as to make everything clear to you. Duncan arrived, and nothing could be more civil than he was. He went out of his way to be nice to everybody and praised the castle, the situation, the view, and even the birds' nests on the walls! (All this, of course, went straight to my heart.) Donalbain and Malcolm were with him. They, I thought at the time, were not at all well brought up. They had not got their father's manners, and they talked in a loud voice and gave themselves airs.

Duncan had supper by himself, and before he went to bed he sent me a most beautiful diamond ring, which I shall always wear. Then we all went to bed. Macbeth was not himself that evening, and he frightened me out of my wits by talking of ghosts and witches and daggers. I did not, however, think anything serious was the matter and I still put it down to the strain and excitement. However, I took the precaution of pouring a drop or two of my sleeping draught into the glass of water which he always drinks before going to bed, so that at least he might have a good night's rest. I suppose I did not give him a strong enough dose. (But one cannot be too careful with drugs, especially mandragora, which is bad for the heart.) At any rate, whether it was that or the awful weather we had that night (nearly all the trees in the park were blown down, and it will never be quite the same again) or whether it was that the hall porter got tipsy (why they choose the one day in the year to drink when one has guests, and it really matters, I never could understand!) and made the most dreadful noise and used really disgraceful language at the front door about five o'clock in the morning, I don't know. At any rate, we were all disturbed long before I had meant that we should be called (breakfast wasn't nearly ready and Elspeth was only just raking out the fires). But, as I say, we were all woken up, and Macduff went to call the King, and came back with the terrible news.

Macbeth turned quite white, and at first my only thought was for him. I thought he was going to have a stroke or a fit. You know he has a very nervous, high-strung constitution, and nothing could be worse for him than a shock like this. I confess that I myself felt as though I wished the earth would open and swallow me up. To think of such a thing happening in our house!

Banquo, too, was as white as a sheet; but the only people who behaved badly (of course this is strictly between ourselves, and I do implore you not to repeat it, as it would really do harm if it got about that I had said this, but you are safe, aren't you, Flora?) were Donalbain and Malcolm. Donalbain said nothing at all, and all Malcolm said when he was told that his father had been murdered was: "Oh! by whom?" I could not understand how he could behave in such a heartless way before so many people; but I must say in fairness that all the Duncans have a very odd way of showing grief.

Of course the first thing I thought was "Who can have done it?" and I suppose in a way it will always remain a mystery. There is no doubt that the chamber grooms actually did the deed; but whether they had any accomplices, whether it was just the act of drunkards (it turned out that the whole household had been drinking that night and not only the hall porter) or whether they were *instigated* by any one else (of course don't quote me as having suggested such a thing) we shall never know. Much as I dislike Malcolm and Donalbain, and shocking as I think their behaviour has been, and not only shocking but *suspicious,* I should not like any one to think that I suspected them of so awful a crime. It is one thing to be bad-mannered, it is another to be a parricide. However, there is no getting over the fact that by their conduct, by their extraordinary behaviour and flight to England, they made people suspect them.

I have only just now come to the real subject of my letter. At first Macbeth bore up pretty well in spite of the blow, the shock, and the extra worry of the coronation following immediately on all this; but no sooner had we settled down at Forres than I soon saw he was far from being himself.

His appetite was bad; he slept badly, and was cross

to the servants, making scenes about nothing. When I tried to ask him about his health he lost his temper. At last one day it all came out and I realized that another tragedy was in store for us. Macbeth is suffering from hallucinations; this whole terrible business has unhinged his mind. The doctor always said he was highly strung, and the fact is he has had another attack, or whatever it is, the same as he had after the battle, when he thought he had seen three witches. (I afterwards found out from Banquo, who was with him at the time, that the matter was even worse than I suspected.) He is suffering from a terrible delusion. He thinks (of course you will never breathe this to a soul) that he killed Duncan! You can imagine what I am going through. Fortunately, nobody has noticed it.

Only last night another calamity happened. Banquo had a fall out riding and was killed. That night we had a banquet we could not possibly put off. On purpose I gave strict orders that Macbeth was not to be told of the accident until the banquet was over, but Lennox (who has no more discretion than a parrot) told him, and in the middle of dinner he had another attack, and I had only just time to get every one to go away before he began to rave. As it was, it must have been noticed that he wasn't himself.

I am in a terrible position. I never know when these fits are coming on, and I am afraid of people talking, because if it once gets about, people are so spiteful that somebody is sure to start the rumour that it's true. Imagine our position, then! So I beg you, dear Flora, to keep all this to yourself, and if possible to come here as soon as possible.

I am, your affectionate,
Harriet R.

P.S.—*Don't* forget to bring Jeamie. It will do Macbeth good to see a child in the house.

Yscolan

by Myrddyn,
translated by W.S. Merwin

*By the end of the play, Macbeth realizes
that although the witches' prophesies
were true in the literal sense, they led him
to damnation. In the following Welsh
poem, written in the sixth century, a seer
declares that he too was misled into doing
evil.*

Your horse is black your cloak is black
your face is black you are black
you are all black—is it you Yscolan?

I am Yscolan the seer
5   my thoughts fly they are covered with clouds.
Is there no reparation then for offending the
    Master?

I burned a church I killed the cows that
    belonged to a school
I threw the Book into the waves
my penance is heavy.

10   Creator of living things you
greatest of all my protectors forgive me.
He that betrayed you deceived me.

I was fastened for a whole year
at Bangor under the piles of the dam.
15 Try to think what I suffered from the sea
    worms.

If I had known what I know now
the liberty of the wind in the moving tree tops
that crime could not be laid to me.